Overthinking Everything, Especially You:
Stop the Spiral and Start Feeling Safe in Love

Bilal Kosovac, LMHC

1

Table of Contents

Introduction

When one thinks of a healthy relationship, a few key points or images may come up. You may imagine a partnership in which your companion is there to support you whenever you struggle, or someone that you can laugh with for hours, without a care in the world. Your image of the perfect relationship may be one in which your partner is a great parent, a true partner with whom you share all your thoughts, worries, and the responsibilities you have as a couple. Or, you may be a bit more traditional, and see a perfect relationship as one in which the male is the provider, and the female is the one who takes care of the home and raises the kids. Regardless of your view of this "perfect relationship," and regardless of the differences between yours and someone else's relationship, there will always be a few things in common when this relationship is healthy: you feel secure, and you trust that your partner will respect their vow to protect your heart.

Right, so this may sound pretty poetic. But in reality, the truth is that most people's relationships do not actually look all this perfect. Most relationships are, in fact, pretty rocky! A big reason for this? The fact that we tend to overthink them.

We overthink whether this is the right partner for us, whether what they say is really what they think, whether we are choosing the right person, whether this is "the one," and the list goes on. Of course, there are many reasons why this happens, and one of the reasons is that we are fed images of what the perfect relationship is like from a very young age. You may not have realized it when you were younger, but watching Disney movies may very well have affected your perspective of what the "perfect relationship" is. Is it when the prince charming wakes up the princess from her deep sleep? When the male protagonist runs throughout the entire city to find out who the slipper belongs to? Or, are we expecting too much from normal people who may not have the capability to fulfill all our hopes and dreams?

Beyond the movies and Disney depictions of love, there are many other reasons why we may overthink our relationships. For example, with social media, we are constantly fed a narrative around what the "right" behavior is for a partner, what constitutes "toxic behavior," and so on. How do we understand what's real from what's fad or trendy on TikTok? How do we know what is really concerning about a partner, and what is just a part of them

4

that we have to learn to love and appreciate? And how do we stop overthinking it?

In your relationship, overthinking may also, and most primarily, look like this. You may imagine that your partner is lying to you, that they aren't saying things how they really are, or that they are "too good to be true," so you wait for the ball to drop (especially if you have a history of being in unhealthy relationships). It may also look like being afraid of being hurt or abandoned, so you overthink your partner's every action, trying to decipher what the real meaning behind them is. It may look like not trusting them when they say they were out with friends, and questioning them endlessly about them, even if you notice them getting annoyed, and even if you know that your questions are irrational. It may also look like trying to control things that you cannot control because they are external.

Overthinking is a complex issue. It is something that can completely ruin relationships, because there is only so much reassurance that partners can do. It is draining, both for you and your partner, because the more you overthink, the more convinced you become about the things you assume are true, and the more you become concerned with discerning whether they are true or not. This all takes a toll on your relationship, and especially on your partner. But overthinking is complex because it can't just be fixed by something as simple as "going on a walk" or "stopping overthinking" (no, don't worry, this book will not give you these tips because guess what, if they worked, you wouldn't be reading this book!). Overthinking takes time to get past, and often some therapy. It takes gaining a greater understanding of the reasons why you overthink, even when you know that you are overthinking and that there is nothing actually happening beyond the surface of the situation at hand.

Overthinking is also something that emerges from the kind of attachment style you have. Though we will dive deeper into this topic in the upcoming chapters, here's a quick description. Your attachment style mainly stems from the kind of childhood you have had, especially the attachment you had to your parents. If you had a parent who made you feel like you had to work to earn their love and appreciation, you may have an anxious attachment style. If you had an absent parent, one that traveled a lot, or were abandoned by a parent when you were young, you may have an avoidant attachment style, whereby you dismiss partners out of fear of letting people get closer to you because this is how they can hurt you. If you were often fearful of your parents, or if you experienced some form of childhood trauma, neglect, or abuse, you may have a disorganized attachment style, in which you might seek love, but may also push your partner away because you fear it. And finally, if none of these apply to you, and if you grew up in a loving and affectionate home, you may have a secure attachment type. This doesn't mean that you won't overthink, but it may make it slightly less likely, because you don't see the point of overthinking something when someone tells you something, you know that people can be trusted, and you know how to spot people who aren't trustworthy, so you don't get into relationships with them! The bottomline is that your attachment style will greatly impact your tendencies to overthink.

This book is here to help you make a change. If you are tired of struggling in your relationships, or the current partnership you are in, then this book is for you. I have years of experience working with people who, like you, have struggled to understand why they overthink, and why they care so much about something they aren't able to control. I am here, writing this book today, to give you solutions to the problem, and to help you ditch your overthinking patterns for good. To do this, we will start by looking at the reasons why we overthink, namely by starting with a chapter that will help you understand your overthinking patterns. Then, we will jump into attachment theory, which is where I will be expanding on the attachment styles described briefly abroad. We will explore each attachment style in more detail, as this greatly impacts why you overthink, and hence, how you can stop doing so. We will also explore how this is formed, and how this influences your relationship.

Of course, this book wouldn't be complete without clear solutions. So, we will be exploring different ways you can try overcoming your overthinking patterns, such as by understanding your triggers, using mindfulness in times of stress, how you can communicate better in moments when you feel like you are overthinking, how you can reframe negative thought patterns to change your ways of thinking and the actions that come as a result, how you can set healthy boundaries that help you and your partner treat each other with respect and in a way that helps you avoid overthinking, and much more.

This is a journey that will require you to be kind to yourself. Overthinking can be overwhelming, because sometimes, you feel like you are working against your brain. So, we are all about self-care here! This is another technique we will be exploring, alongside welcoming imperfection and your ability to grow, as well as rebuilding trust, connection, and forgiving yourself to heal from your past and/or your current experiences. This book is here to help you start your journey towards a life, and especially an experience with relationships, that is free of overthinking.

It may feel impossible at the moment. You might have picked up this book thinking that it won't help, or that like other self-help books, you will end up with a few new pieces of knowledge but no way to truly apply them. But as a working therapist, my job and passion in life is to help you and couples (perhaps like yours) feel more secure and move on with more certainty and confidence.

Are you ready to make some changes to your relationship and life? Are you ready to put an end to your overthinking patterns for good?

Let's get started!

Chapter One

Understanding Overthinking

Having briefly discussed what overthinking is, it's time to explore this in more detail. You might have heard of overthinking on social media, but unfortunately, in this day and age, we tend to hear many buzzwords (and use them) without really understanding what they actually refer to. This chapter aims to put an end to this. If you are reading this book, it is because you are personally greatly affected by overthinking, so you deserve to understand what it truly means in great detail.

The Basics of Overthinking

Starting with the basics, let's give it a definition. Overthinking is when your thoughts are stuck in a loop.

This refers to the act of overthinking a situation or problem, such as overthinking a role (i.e., employment), a situation (e.g., doing a presentation, or sitting an exam), or overthinking in a relationship, which is the main topic of discussion in the context of this book. When we overthink, we simply think about something too much, or for too long, beyond its productive level. In other words, we think about something so much that it becomes unproductive, because we think about it to the extent that it does not bring us anything anymore. You may have been told by friends, family, or even your partner to "stop overthinking this" because to them, the solution or outcome of thinking about that very thing is clear and simple, but to you, it is not. You want to think things through again and again, even if you come to the very same conclusion that you would come to if you only thought about it so much.

In the context of your relationship, overthinking happens when we worry too much about something. We might analyze, and ruminate over something endlessly, and then, we get anxious about it. The "What If's" start, but what if this, and what if that? We think, think, and think some more, and we get into a vicious cycle of analyzing all the potential outcomes or scenarios, even if most of them are extremely unlikely, or even impossible!

For example, you might overthink about the relationship itself. You might question whether this is the kind of relationship that you want, and whether the person ticks all your boxes. You may compare your relationship to that of your friends. You may analyze what your partner does, how you act in the relationship, whether this is the kind of relationship that you have seen in the movies, whether your partner is fitting the boxes you want them to fit in, whether it's the kind of relationship you think your parents would approve of, whether your friends would approve of the relationship, whether you are the "power couple" you want to be, and the list goes on. You might also overthink your partner, are they smart enough? Do they make you laugh enough? Are they rich enough? Do they fit your boxes and what you expect in a partner? Are they telling the truth when they say they went somewhere? Are they really in love with you, or do they just say that to make you happy? Do they make you happy, or does the relationship make you happy? Do they dress well enough? How do your friends view them? Do you look like you have "won" with this relationship? What do other people think? What about your partner's friends, do they like you? Or, you might overthink the interactions you have within this relationship, where you think about the texts they have sent, you question whether they like you back, whether they are going to ghost you, whether they are actually interested in you, whether you text them too much, whether you are too clingy, and so on.

Don't get me wrong, it's normal to have a bit of anxiety at the start of the relationship, where you wonder whether this is the right person for you, whether they are actually interested in you or whether you are reading their cues the wrong way, or whether you are seeing this relationship as something other than what it really is. This is normal at the start, you are trying to figure this person out, trying to understand who they are, how they think, and how they act. But the problems start when this goes beyond the initial dating days, when you know them, when you have communicated with them, when they know what you expect and vice versa, and when you constantly wonder whether they are really telling the truth or whether they are lying to you. This is where we shift from typical nervousness or even excitement about a new relationship, and irrational overthinking.

The Characteristics of Overthinking

In the context of a relationship, overthinking can take many forms. It can, for example, take the form of constantly worrying about the state of your relationship or your partner's feelings. You may know deep down that they mean what they say when they say I Love You, but you may irrationally question whether they actually mean it or not. You might even think that they are lying to you and just saying these things out loud to please you, when in reality, they mean every word of it. Otherwise, it can also look like constantly analyzing and re-analyzing the conversations you have between each other, the actions they take and whether they really follow what they say, the intentions they have versus the ones they say they have, and so on. You may already see how exhausting this can be for both you and your partner, for you because your mind constantly makes you wonder whether things are going well between you two, or whether the ball is about to drop, and for your partner, because they may feel this silent pressure that they constantly have to reaffirm their feelings and intentions to you. And, even then, you might keep questioning them! You don't mean to, but this is nonetheless the outcome you are dealing with.

This is another characteristic of overthinking, you might struggle to accept things at face value, and instead, you might look for hidden meanings or signs in your partner's behavior. This is exhausting to do, and you might even ask yourself, "why can't I just trust what I hear?" This is what overthinking does, it starts a cycle, a trap, in which you feel like what you hear is never the full story, even when it is.

The Forms of Overthinking

Likewise, overthinking can take many forms! You might ruminate, which is where you constantly think about the same worries, the same past events, or the same past conflicts. This inevitably can make you sad, or even lead to depression, because it keeps your mind stuck in a cycle where you constantly think about what could be going wrong, what is going wrong, what might go wrong, and so on. This isn't a healthy way of thinking for anybody, but for someone who overthinks, it's a gateway to constantly feeling sad and not knowing how to get past it.

You may also worry constantly, which is different from rumination. When you ruminate, you think a lot, but this isn't necessarily always negative. It can just be thinking. When you worry, there is a level of stress that comes with it. You might be worried about negative outcomes, bad things happening in your relationship, or fear the worst in the future scenarios you imagine about your relationship. For example, when meeting someone new and going on a few dates, instead of enjoying your time with them, you might constantly think about the potential negative outcomes, breaking up, being heartbroken, cheating, etc, without thinking about the positives too. Your brain far prefers jumping to negative outcomes than thinking about what could happen that could make you happy. This is a normal part of human nature, as we have something called a negativity bias.

The negativity bias is what researchers refer to when discussing the "way that adults use positive versus negative information to make sense of their world." The following explains this well:

"At a higher cognitive level, negative stimuli are hypothesized to carry greater informational value than positive stimuli, and to thus require greater attention and cognitive processing (see Peeters & Czapinski, 1990). Accordingly, adults spend more time looking at negative than at positive stimuli, perceive negative stimuli to be more complex than positive ones, and form more complex cognitive representations of negative than of positive stimuli (e.g., Ducette & Soucar, 1974; Fiske, 1980; H. Miller & Bieri, 1965)."

In simple words, this means that whenever we receive a negative stimulus, we tend to pay more attention to it than when we feel a positive stimulus. So, when we have negative thoughts, or when we worry about something potentially negative, it is hard for our brains to focus on the positive because we are greatly anchored on the negatives happening around us. When we think of it further, it makes sense! When positive things happen, we have little to worry about. Things are going well, so we do not have any reason to worry about our safety, whether physical, emotional, or psychological. But when we are worried, that's all we can focus on until our brains can return to feeling safe and sound. However, when we overthink, we constantly have the negativity bias on, whatever negative outcome we think could happen, we take it at full speed, focus on it, hyperfixate on it, think of it in a thousand different ways, and then the cycle continues.

Much of this overthinking is fuelled by self-doubt. You might question your own worthiness, your compatibility, whether you can satisfy your partner, or whether you are enough. And yet, you have little, if not no evidence at all, that this is true. I have seen first-hand how many relationships end as a result of one person's self-doubts and lack of self-worth, and this is because these issues can cause a huge strain on the relationship. One person doubting that they are worthy of love can make it extremely difficult for the other to cope with, because constantly needing to convince the other person that they are worthy of love, that they are lovable, and of course, that they are loved, is draining. Likewise, convincing another person that their doubts are unfounded is tiring and can quickly become overwhelming for the other partner, which can lead to the destruction of the relationship over time.

What Triggers Overthinking?

Now, what makes all this happen? For many partners, overthinking may stem from a lack of communication. As a result, assumptions start arising, and either partner may wonder whether they have misunderstood something, whether they are in the wrong, and so on. Communication goes both ways. So, a lack of communication from the overthinker's side can just as much be at fault. For example, miscommunicating expectations can lead them to feel like they aren't heard or respected all while the other partner has no idea that any of this is happening. Assumptions is also where miscommunication comes in, and it can lead to fights in which both partners have entirely different points of view and pick at each other while being on entirely different wavelengths.

Past traumas or insecurities could also affect current relationship dynamics and are a breeding ground for overthinking. For example, let's say that the overthinker has experienced a very toxic relationship in the past. Their previous partner was constantly gaslighting them, lying to them, and making themselves out to be someone entirely different. They were emotionally abusive and used intimacy

18

as another way to make their partner subservient by being caring and affectionate only during this time. The result? The victim in this relationship, now in a new relationship, struggles to avoid being anxious or nervous around their new partner because they worry that this new partner is lying, or is only going to turn out to be the same person.

And finally, social media can work as a trigger, too! We constantly see other people online, showcasing their relationships, their incredible lives running around in beautiful vacation spots, highlighting their perfect kids going to the best schools, and as a result, we can get discouraged. Do these people never argue? Do they always agree on everything? Do they not miscommunicate sometimes? Why does my relationship look so different? Why don't we go on endless vacations too? Why doesn't my partner buy me a bed of roses when I come back from a trip? Why does she not show me as much affection as I see other people online talking about? Is it me, am I the problem?

These are all kinds of triggers that can influence your overthinking patterns. How to overcome these is what we will be discussing in upcoming chapters.

The Roots of Overthinking: Fear, Insecurity, and Past Experiences

Let's explore where overthinking stems from in a bit more detail. We have looked at the triggers briefly, but the root causes of overthinking stem from far beyond this. Specifically, overthinking tends to stem from fear, insecurities, and past experiences. Understanding these is the starting point for your journey towards changing your overthinking patterns, so let's have a look!

First, there is fear. This can be a fear of many things. You might fear losing something, or someone. For example, you might fear losing your relationship and dealing with the aftermath of this. We have all been heartbroken before, and we know how taxing it can be on us. We feel a hot feeling of pain in our hearts, like our hearts physically hurt. We feel depressed, as though we will never experience true happiness ever again. It is a loss that we grieve. We may not have lost someone entirely, they are still alive after all, but it feels like it. This person will never be part of our lives the same way that they were before. Feeling like this is scary, so we might overthink things in our relationship because it feels like we are protecting ourselves in a way. By overthinking the potential scenarios, we mentally feel like we are prepared for what's to come. But of course, this is draining for our partner, who may feel like we are constantly thinking about the worst case scenarios, without considering the potential positive outcomes!

We may also fear rejection. As human beings, it is normal for us to want to be loved and wanted. It is part of our nature to want to protect ourselves from rejection because previously, we needed to be accepted as part of a community to survive. Thousands of years ago, as we fought off tigers and lions in the middle of the night, part of our survival was entirely dependent on having other people there to keep watch in the middle of the night and to wake us up if we had to fight. So, being rejected from the tribe was equivalent to a death sentence. Well, we may no longer need to fight off tigers (at least most of us), but we still have a lasting need to be accepted. So, fear of rejection is natural, but overthinking it when we are constantly reminded by our partner that we have nothing to fear is where the problem lies. If we are constantly concerned of being rejected, or not being good enough for our partner, we might end up overanalyzing interactions so we can detect hints of their interest starting to wane.

Finally, we may fear conflict. This is especially the case for those with unhealthy attachment patterns who may try to avoid conflict at all costs, including productive and healthy conflict that leads to a positive resoltuion. You might overthink and second-guess your feelings or your responses, and you might even put your own wishes and needs aside for the sake of protecting yourself and ensuring that no conflict takes place, ever. Perhaps you grew up in an environment in which conflicts always led to altercations, screaming, shouting matches, and negative outcomes, so you now automatically attach "conflict" to "negativity." But in reality, conflict is not always this chaotic, and it is even necessary at times to make sure that both you and your partner are on the same page. It might sound scary, but trust me, conflict doesn't have to end badly!

Second, there is insecurity. We already covered how self-doubt can lead to overthinking simple situations, but so can a low level of self-esteem. If you feel like you aren't worthy of great love, you may accept poor treatment from people, and you may also end up in relationships with people who are amazingly loving but who you think you do not deserve. They may constantly tell you that they love you, but you cannot be convinced. Nor should you be, it isn't your partner's job to convince you that you are lovable, you should come into this relationship with the belief that you are lovable, and that you do deserve to be treated in a certain way! This low self-esteem can be draining not just for you but for your partner too, because you may constantly need reassurance, or you might overinterpret your partner's actions and think that they aren't happy with you, that they do not love you, and so on.

Attachment issues fall in this category as well. If you have an insecure attachment style, whether that's avoidant or anxious, you can end up overthinking your entire relationship, which may lead you to either cling or distance yourself from your partner, whether it's because you are worried you will be abandoned, or worried that the person will hurt you if you let them in.

Third, and somewhat related, your previous experiences can be at the root of your overthinking. As mentioned earlier, a traumatic experience with a partner can lead you to doubt what people say, to fear being lied to, or to be worried that the same experience will happen again. Maybe you were betrayed in the past, or maybe you were abandoned, and this can (very naturally!) cause you to lack trust with your new partner. You just want to avoid getting hurt again, and this is a normal reaction for anyone having experienced something similar! Your childhood influences will also affect this, namely by affecting your attachment style and the expected treatment you have for relationships. For example, if you grew up with an abusive or narcissistic parent who constantly made you feel like you had to earn their love, it's only normal that you would reproduce this expectation in your romantic relationships. Finally, you may have grown up in an environment in which overthinking was normal, which may be why you have continued the habit.

The Cycle of Overthinking: How It Works, and Why It Hurts Your Relationships

Overthinking is a cycle. In fact, it can create a self-fulfilling prophecy, which is where what you say will happen does happen because of the actions you take, even if it never would have happened in the first place had you acted differently. In other words, the more you overthink, the more you reinforce the fears and insecurities that are driving your overthinking, which creates a vicious cycle. So, the goal for this book is to help you break that cycle, and to help you identify ways to spot when you are overthinking so you can mindfully put an end to it.

Recognizing Overthinking Patterns and Their Effects!

Overthinking Patterns

As a final note for this chapter, let's have a look at a few patterns that you can notice when you overthink. For example, as mentioned earlier, rumination is one of the most common patterns you may notice when overthinking. If you notice yourself thinking over the same worries again and again, and feeling increasingly anxious the more you think, take a moment to acknowledge the fact that you are ruminating. Alongside this, catastrophizing is another common pattern. This is when you imagine the worst potential scenarios, regardless of whether the situation is actually minor, or whether it is even something to worry about at all. In these instances, even the smallest of situations, like having a disagreement with your partner, could make you feel like the worst possible outcome is about to happen. You may think that you are about to break up, that your partner no longer loves you, and so on.

Another pattern is mind reading, which is when you assume what your partner is thinking, what they are feeling, or what they want to do, all without asking them for their perspective. This inevitably will lead to misunderstandings, but it also leads you to be upset about something that isn't necessarily true. If you aren't sure of what your partner said, thinks, or did, ask them!

Likewise, if you look for reassurance very often, this is a sign that you may be overthinking your relationship. If you never feel convinced by your partner's words, actions, or promises they make to you, and if you constantly would like them to give you more reassurance, to make you feel better about yourself, take a moment to realize that this is an overthinking pattern. Unless your partner has shown you otherwise, you should be able to trust their words and what they show you.

Finally, pay attention to your expectations, whether this is an expectation for yourself, or for your partner. Relationships are not perfect. They have ups and downs, they have conflict, and they will sometimes be challenging. The same is true for your partner, there is no such thing as a perfect partner. You cannot be perfect either. So, don't hold yourself, or your partner, to unrealistically high standards! This will only lead you to be dissatisfied with your relationship and/or your partner, and it can make your partner feel like they are never able to fulfill your needs or requirements.

Effects of Overthinking

Overthinking is exhausting for you and your partner. It makes you more and more anxious, stressed, and as we have seen, it can lead you to overthink and struggle with depression. It can also lead to "paralysis by analysis," which is when you struggle to make a decision because your mind is overwhelmed with the amount of information it is trying to compute. Likewise, you might be very worried about making the wrong decision, so you avoid making a decision at all to avoid the potentially negative outcome. This can make your relationship stagnate entirely because of your lack of ability to make a decision that could lead to growth and better, newer things.

But overthinking has very real impacts for your self-esteem and even your physical health, too. Constantly doubting yourself, criticizing yourself, and thinking that you aren't good enough is tough on you, no one deserves to deal with these kinds of negative thinking patterns! You deserve to be kind to yourself, and doing the opposite just reinforces negative thinking patterns. Your physical health suffers from it too, the chronic stress that comes from constantly overthinking your situation takes a toll on you, and chronic stress has been shown to lead to all kinds of other issues including insomnia, headaches, digestive problems, and many more!

But more related to the context of this book, overthinking pacts your relationship both in the short and long terms. The more you overthink, the more likely you are to be dealing with miscommunication, assumptions, conflicts that feel like they never really get resolved, and more. When you overthink, the conflicts feel like they are never-ending because even though you have both come to an agreement, you are still not fully convinced. You keep thinking it through, over and over again, and never come to a conclusion that feels satisfying. So, you may bring the conflict back up, in the hopes that this time, you will get the closure that you are seeking. But unfortunately, this is a cycle, and no matter what your partner tells you, you will never truly be satisfied with their answer, as long as you still feel insecure in the relationship and continue the cycle of overthinking.

With fights that never get fully resolved, you may start to distance yourselves from one another emotionally. This is where overthinking becomes a self-fulfilling prophecy, your fears have made you act in a way that makes these fears the reality. You may also be the only one who is emotionally distant, and you may therefore withdraw yourself emotionally or physically from your relationship so you can cope, or so you have a feeling of control. While this may give you a false sensation of control, it only makes the relationship deteriorate further.

Your tendency to overthink may also make you more dependent on your partner and their ability to reinforce their love for you. The more you need to be reassured, the more you continue to associate reassurance with a positive and healthy relationship. But this is, you guessed it, tiring for a partner. Remember, a healthy relationship is one in which you feel secure and where you are partners, and a partner is not one-sided, whereby one of the partners is entirely dependent on the other's reassurance for their feeling of self-worth.

Overall, overthinking brings a cycle of negativity into your relationship. Your environment, burdened by a need to be reassured, to feel in control, and to be absolutely certain of your partner's feelings for you, can make it difficult for the two of you to have positive interactions. The result? A relationship that has an expiration date.

By now, you should have a far more developed idea of what overthinking consists of. What we need to establish next is how this comes to be. The more you know about the reasons behind your overthinking patterns, the better equipped you are to take the steps you need to confront this aspect of yourself and to take control (ironically) of the situation. Yes, this is something you can control, unlike many of the situations you may overthink. So, let's focus on what we can change, shall we?

Chapter Two

Attachment Theory

The way we show our love to people, and the people that we get attached to, although not prescribed by our past, is very much influenced by the kind of attachment that we know and are used to. Think of it this way. A person who grows up in a family where love was only given under certain circumstances, and not under others, may grow up with the thought that it is normal to have to do something to receive love. For example, if your mother only showed love for you when you did something specific, but then would rage uncontrollably in other circumstances without any specific trigger, you may have learned that although there are moments of great joy, love, and happiness in a relationship, it is normal that sometimes, unexpected rage happens. And yet, this is not what constitutes a healthy relationship. A healthy relationship is, instead, one in which you know that you are loved and treated with respect no matter what, and that the love you receive will not be conditional. Of course, this is applicable within the bounds of normalcy; you wouldn't be expected to continue being in love with someone who cheats on you, although this isn't the topic of this book.

This chapter focuses on attachment theory, which explains why we, as adults, tend to love and attach ourselves in a way that is either reminiscent of the way we were attached to our parents in childhood, and/or to the way that we love now as a result of a lack of attachment. Originally proposed by John Bowlby, and then expanded upon by Mary Ainsworth, this theory is a great way to better understand why you may overthink in your relationships, as, as we have seen, much of the overthinking we do is attributable to the experiences we had in the past, whether this is with your parents, in past relationships, or both.

Understanding Attachment Theory

Attachment theory was, as mentioned above, introduced by John Bowlby and later on expanded on by Mary Ainsworth. Initially, Bowlby introduced the concept, explaining that as human beings, we have an innate need to form strong emotional bonds with our caregivers, mainly our parents or guardians. These bonds, in turn, affect how we are able to bond with other adults later on in life. Then,

Ainsworth's work, called "Strange Situation" expanded upon this work by developing a procedure in which one could observe attachment relationships between a child and their caregivers. As a result, we now have a classification for attachment styles.

There are a few key elements and principles to explore within this theory. First, the element of early experiences. While growing up, you may have seen how certain children at school seemed better dressed than others, or how certain children had parents that seemed to be more present than others. Perhaps you were the child who noticed this because, for you, seeing other school children being picked up early by their mothers and fathers was drastically different from your own experience. Maybe you were used to the opposite, being left at school longer in the evening, wondering whether your mom or dad had forgotten you. You may have also been shocked to see how your friends would act with their parents and vice versa, maybe you even wondered why your mom doesn't give you as many hugs, or why they don't get yelled at by their dad when they fall and cry.

The experiences we have with our caregivers as children greatly affect how we think we should be treated and handled by adults in our adult lives. If we grow up with absent parents, we grow up to assume that this is the kind of attachment that we are supposed to have. On the other hand, if we grow up with parents who are there to reassure us, to make us feel better, to make us feel happier, and to console us when we feel sad, angry, or down, without reacting in a negative way, we grow up to assume that that is the right way to be treated, and this is the kind of love that we expect from people. Likewise, if we grow up with parents who make us feel like we aren't good enough, or like we need to earn their love, we tend to replicate this expectation when the time comes to meet a partner in life. There are many problems associated with this, it lands people in hot waters when toxic individuals find people with insecure attachment styles, because it makes it easy for the insecure person to be manipulated into thinking that being mistreated, or needing to prove something to be loved, is ok. If this is your case, if you feel like you constantly need to prove your "worthiness" to be loved, you have some work to do. And hey, there are good news! You reading this book is part of that work.

Indeed, this is another core principle of attachment theory, namely that as a result of our early childhood experiences, we develop internal representations of ourselves and others, and these representations guide our future social and romantic relationships. A person with very absent parents, for example, may see themselves as unworthy of being given attention, or of being loved altogether, but they may also feel like the second they allow someone into their lives (or their heart), this person is going to leave. So, they avoid being attached altogether. On the other hand, a person with an anxious attachment style may do everything in their power to remain close to the person, and to prove their worthiness, because they feel that they are only entitled to love if they do what the other person wants them to do. This is usually accompanied by a negative self-view, being worried that you will be abandoned or rejected, and feeling unworthy of a person's love.

A third element of attachment theory is the need for proximity. We all want to feel close to other people. We all want to feel loved, wanted, accepted, and needed. But there is a range that is 'acceptable' or 'healthy,' and outside of that range, it can be unhealthy. It can lead to dependency on another person, or depending on their constant reassurance, as we have seen. But proximity, in general, is something that we all seek, starting from an early age. As newborns, we seek it to feel safe with our parents, because we are unable to fend for ourselves. Then, as we grow up and get older, we also depend on our friends and family as a way to feel that we have a solid support system. Later on, in our romantic relationships, we also want to depend on our partner to feel secure, but being too dependent is where the problems start. We seek proximity, but if we need it from our partners at all costs, and if our sense of self-worth and confidence depends on it, that's when the problems begin.

As a side note, we also need to mention a certain behavior that often comes alongside an anxious attachment. People-pleasing behaviors can also result from early experiences and guide these social and romantic relationships. People-pleasing emerges from the need to constantly prove to people that you are worthy of being loved. It often results from feeling like you needed to prove that you were worthy of love as a child, and hence, doing anything and everything possible to receive this love from people. You may, for example, find yourself often feeling like you do a lot for people around you, even going as far as putting your own needs aside, just to feel like people appreciate you and see you as the person who is always there for others. You may also have gotten into relationships where you always did what you thought the other person wanted you to do, because doing it this way made sure that they would always be happy. And yet, you may also have felt like nothing you ever did was enough. You may avoid conflicts to keep the peace and avoid upsetting someone. You may be afraid of being seen as "mean." This kind of thinking also originates from an anxious attachment style, where you are worried that someone will not like you, so you do everything in your power, and overthink most of it, to keep them at peace.

The Four Attachment Styles

Let's jump right into more detailed descriptions of the attachment styles. As mentioned in the introduction, attachment styles can be categorized as secure, anxious, avoidant, and disorganized. They each emerge from different experiences while growing up, among other things, and they heavily influence how likely we are to be overthinkers.

Let's start with the healthiest attachment style, which is the secure attachment style. This is a style that is positive in that you view yourself and others positively. You are comfortable with intimacy, which reaches far beyond physical intimacy, but includes emotional intimacy too, and you are able to ask for and provide support when needed. The 'ask for' part is important here. When you have a secure attachment style, you do not feel threatened by needing to ask for help. You feel like asking for help is simply another part of life, and that being able to rely on people for their help and support is a great aspect of having that support system available to you. With this attachment style, you view yourself positively. You know that you have great qualities, that you are a great person that people love, that you are appreciated, and that even if you have weaknesses or "faults," that people still like you. You are also in line with the fact that some people might not like you, and that it's not a problem, because not everyone will like everyone. You also see other people as kind and good first, and you may not automatically assume that people might hurt you if you get into a relationship with them, or even if they are just your friend. You also view relationships positively, they can add to your life, but they do not constitute your life as a whole. In your view, a partner is someone that you choose to share your life with, but they do not take too much space, they just add the fun spice and sparkle to it.

Your communication skills, as a secure attachment person, are excellent. You can communicate effectively, and you feel like you are understood and understand others easily, without being confused or worried that they are saying something other than what they think. So, you also do not need constant reassurance, you go by the default that whatever that person is saying must be true, and therefore, that you can trust them. You also don't feel ashamed to express your needs and your feelings openly, and you don't feel anxious if the person you are speaking to disagrees with you or seems to have a different opinion. To you, conflict is something that's necessary sometimes to make sure that everyone's needs and wishes are respected and, importantly, are supported. When your relationships are challenged, you can also ask for help, or you can help your partner. You do not feel like every conflict or disagreement might end up in a larger fight, or might even lead to a breakup. For example, when there are problems in the relationship, you feel comfortable discussing them with your partner. When you have disagreements, you discuss them directly, and you let your partner speak to make sure that they feel heard and respected throughout the conversation. You also make sure that you are working towards a mutual solution and that you are maintaining an emotional closeness between the two of you, no matter what happens, because your partner's wellbeing and emotional safety are important, but importantly, because you do not feel like yours is at threat.

Next, we have a different style, which is the anxious attachment style. This is very different from the previous style because there is a great lack of security in the person's attachment style. For example, there is the fear of abandonment, which may lead the person to try to tighten the rope to make sure that they are not abandoned. With this attachment style, the mindset is that "if I am scared that they will leave me, I just need to keep them as close to me as possible. This way, I can be sure that they won't be able to leave me, and I can keep proving to them that I am worthy of being loved." There is a similar fear of being rejected, which has the same result, neediness in the relationship, which may infringe on the partner's need for privacy, time alone, or some space. The anxious attachment style is also often associated with a very negative self-view. For example, if you have this style, you may struggle to believe that your partner actually loves you, and you may, instead, feel like they are lying to you or will never be content with who you are and what you have to offer. This mainly stems from a lack of self-esteem, where you may even be bewildered that this person is with you, thinking that you don't deserve them! You may think that they are too good for you, and therefore, that you have to constantly prove to them that you are worthy of their love, and that they should not leave you.

Otherwise, you may indeed be overly concerned that they will stop loving you, that they will stop showing interest, or that if you do not keep giving them attention, showing your interest, and the like, that they will go to someone else. You may be worried when they do not reply quickly enough, thinking that this may be because they aren't interested anymore, or because they do not want you. Often, this kind of attachment is also personalized, instead of seeing this as a person who is not interested in general, you automatically assume that there is something wrong with you personally. So, when you are in a relationship with them, you have a tendency to ask for reassurance often, and in many ways. You want validation that your fears are unfounded.

You may ask for it very often, because hearing it once is not convincing enough. You may feel like this person is lying to you, or is not telling you the whole truth, and you may want to intrude on their privacy, looking through their messages, having their location, etc, to convince yourself that you have nothing to worry about. You are also very sensitive, overly sensitive, to your partner's moods and actions, where you may think that them not showing you attention 24/7 shows a lack of interest, when in fact, your partner may simply be busy. If they are angry, you may fear the worst, and if they lack excitement, you may feel like they are just not that interested.

The third kind of attachment style is the avoidant attachment style, which is often seen in cases where one is hyper independent. This is because the avoidant style often results from a person needing to be independent early on in their lives, and therefore making this their normality and what they assume is best. There is a specific emphasis on independence, whereby you dislike having to rely on someone else to do something for you, you do not appreciate it, because you feel like depending on someone makes you more vulnerable, and more likely to be let down by others.

So, you are a very self-sufficient person, and you don't want to rely on someone else to help you out, or to give you any kind of support. Actually, that makes you uncomfortable! In a similar vein, you feel uncomfortable with closeness and especially vulnerability in your relationships. To you, it feels like someone is intruding in your space, and is taking up some space that you don't feel completely comfortable sharing yet, because being open means being vulnerable. So, you may be emotionally distant from your partner, and you may have a hard time expressing your emotions or welcoming theirs, much to their dismay. They may in fact have told you this many times, and may have told you that they aren't happy with the lack of affection you provide them with.

There is an important difference here, which is that you have a positive view of yourself, but you are not trustful of others' intentions and whether they are reliable. You might think along the lines of "I've been burned in the past" so you choose to avoid ever being close to a flame again, this way, it is safer, and you do not need to worry about ever being hurt by someone's bad actions or intentions again.

41

You avoid discussing your feelings, and you absolutely do everything in your power to avoid relying on other people, you like to solve your problems on your own. This may have manifested in your previous relationships, too. For example, you may have felt uncomfortable before when your partner asked you to open up and to share your emotions with them, and you may often be told that you walk away when the conversation gets tough. You might also often quit relationships before they even start, because you feel like the phase where you need to open up and share your emotions or feelings is already too vulnerable. So, although you want to love and be loved, it's extremely difficult for you to do so, because you come at it with the perspective that the person is there to harm you, or that they will inevitably harm you in the future.

The final type is the disorganized attachment style. This is a mix of the two. It is a type that we see a lot in people who experienced childhood traumas and who grew up never knowing whether their caregiver would be present and caring, or whether they would not be (e.g., neglectful parents). This is characterized by a specific mix of anxious and avoidant behaviors, which can make it confusing for your partner, particularly due to the inconsistencies. For example, you might struggle to trust your partner because you view others as potentially harmful, and because you view yourself as unworthy of love or respect. Likewise, you might show signs of being clingy and distant, and this is typically unpredictable. So, for example, you may show a lot of interest sometimes, and at other times, if the interest is shown back to you, you may pull back in fears that the person isn't being truthful or honest. You might also be clingy at times, and other times, may want to be hyper independent, while your partner feels like they are mostly in the way of your plans and schedule. This can be tiring for the partner as they may not know what to expect.

As you can see, attachment styles change us, and how we view relationships, tremendously. So, naturally, they also affect our relationships as a whole! Although we didn't discuss it above, insecure attachment styles often lead to a lot of overthinking, whether it is because one is anxious about the relationship, is worried they will be abandoned because they are too distant, or is fearful of their partner leaving them because they cannot deal with the hot-and-cold treatment anymore. Our attachment styles can lead us to be obsessively worried, to imagining the worst case scenarios. As such, they play a great role in determining who we date, and how the relationship unravels. Let's explore this in more detail.

Your Attachment Style and Relationships Are Connected!

As we have seen, our early attachment experiences shape the kind of expectations we have in the future, and the behaviors we have as adults. As the theory goes, our attachment styles, then, also influences who we end up with, and how satisfied we are with them. For example, a secure attachment style is generally associated with a healthier and more resilient relationship, while the opposite is also true, having an anxious or avoidant attachment is typically associated with more difficulties in a relationship, like miscommunications, emotional distancing, and so on.

Communication

First, let's consider the impact that our attachment styles have on one of the most crucial elements of our relationships: how we communicate. We each have different communication styles, but they all tend to fall within a realm of healthy vs. unhealthy. Healthy communication is that which makes people feel good, which leads to a good outcome, and in which people feel great about themselves. They walk out of a conversation feeling great, fulfilled, and satisfied. They aren't belittled, they aren't worried about the conversation leading to a break up, and they aren't scared that this conversation or conflict will make their partner stop loving them. On the other hand, unhealthy communication is the opposite, passive aggressive, rarely leads to good outcomes, and leaves one or both parties feeling quite down.

For securely attached people, communication comes almost naturally. It's something that they do openly, honestly, and importantly, constructively. Securely attached people see communication as a way for both parties to come together and come to a common understanding of each others' feelings and views of a certain situation or concern. It is something positive, constructive, and something that does not evoke very intense emotions. For anxious individuals, however, communication is far different. It can be overly needy, and in times of conflict, it can make them extremely scared and worried about the outcome. As an anxiously attached person, one may fear that communication is more than what is being said; namely, that the person they are speaking with is withholding how they truly feel, their real emotions and thoughts, and therefore, the conversation might go in circles. Even once the conversation has ended, they may not feel entirely satisfied unless a lot of reassurance has been provided. General communication may be over-the-top, too. For example, they may find it necessary to be in constant contact with their partner, and may worry that a few late texts, or the person not calling as soon as they are available, translates into that person not being interested. Finally, those who have an avoidant attachment style may be more withdrawn and minimal in their communication so as to avoid being vulnerable altogether.

Conflict Resolution

This leads us to the similar element that is affected by our attachment style: conflict resolution. To resolve conflicts in a healthy way, we need healthy conflict resolution skills. Therefore, the more difficult communication is in general, the more strenuous a conflict might be on either or both partners. For example, while a securely attached person might feel like conflicts are just part of life and that they have the potential to lead to a positive outcome, to someone who is anxiously attached, this is a hard notion to grasp. If one grew up in an environment where every conflict led to hurtful words, the person walking out of the room, being punished, being called names, or being mistreated in general, naturally, conflicts become associated with this kind of treatment, no matter which kind of conflict is taking place and who the other person involved is. Likewise, for a person with an avoidant style, conflict may make the person feel like too many emotions are involved, the person is asking too much of them in terms of opening up, and conflict may generally make them feel like they are being pushed in a box where they feel too vulnerable.

Dealing with Stressful Situations

Putting aside communication, emotional regulation and support are two other elements that are influenced by our attachment styles. For example, when it comes to regulating our emotions when we are under stress, we can expect that someone with a secure attachment style will do far better than someone with an anxious attachment style. Someone with a secure attachment style will most likely feel like regardless of the situation they are in, as long as their partners stay open and communicate with them, there is nothing to be worried about, and nothing to overthink about. On the other hand, someone with an anxious attachment style may have coping mechanisms that actually hurt the relationship.

Let's imagine the following. Let's say that you are in a relationship with someone that you have been getting to know for around seven or eight months. All is going well, you know that you have anxious tendencies and that sometimes, you need to take a step back and think. However, you also know that at other times, you feel more anxious than others. On days where things are great, they feel great all around. But when things start feeling a little less great, you start thinking things through.

Let's imagine that this partner of yours tells you that they are going away for a month to travel. At first, things are good, you are excited for them. They are excited to be there. You make time to call and talk every few days and you keep yourself busy for those first days. The first week goes by and it's great, you are communicative, your partner makes an effort to keep you updated, all is good. And then, more time starts going by.

You learn that they are hanging out with people from the opposite sex (if you are in a heterosexual relationship, if not, apply this to your relationship), you hear that they are having a great time, but you feel like the communication isn't quite what you would like it to be. You start wondering what their messages mean. You wonder whether they actually want to call when they ask you whether you are free, or whether they are actually only doing this because they know that it is important to you. You wonder whether your relationship will survive this trip because deep down, you feel like maybe they're interested in other people there, people who want to do the same things as them. You might even feel like the trip will make them think Wow, I don't actually like this person! And then, the spiraling starts. One thought brings another one, and the scenarios begin. You imagine the worst case scenarios, the worst possible things that could happen. You think of them having fun while you aren't having any at all, quite the opposite, actually. But you're also stuck in a position where you can't really expect them to give you the normal amount of attention and consideration because, after all, they're abroad. So, little by little, to protect your heart, once you have past the point of panic, you switch to annoyance and anger and decide not to care anymore. Maybe you can send a passive aggressive message, or maybe you can act coldly towards them.

You could also just not message them and only expect them to message you first. You might tell yourself that you will no longer put in effort, telling yourself that this is to "mirror their actions" when, in reality, you are just trying to protect your heart. It gives you a false sense of control over a situation you can't control. The problem with this way of thinking, however, is that your coping mechanism for the stress you are feeling is entirely one-sided, and it is not something you are sharing with your partner. Additionally, you are spending much more time worrying about things that you cannot confirm, because you aren't checking in with them. You are thinking about all this all by yourself, never checking whether your perspective, view, or what you understand from the situation is truly what it is. So, your coping mechanisms with stress may lead you to engage in toxic behaviors, such as thinking that if you don't contact them, if you are cold, or if you "mirror" the way you perceive they are acting, which can lead to your partner feeling like they are either being manipulated, or just plainly confused! This is a very specific stressful situation, but the same can be applied to other kinds of stressful situations.

Maladaptive Coping Mechanisms

Let's explore the kinds of maladaptive coping mechanisms you may have in more detail. Beyond just being passive aggressive with a partner, you may use other such mechanisms, which are coping strategies that can negatively impact our wellbeing, instead of helping us cope better. There are obvious maladaptive coping mechanisms, such as turning to drugs or alcohol to deal with your stress, but there are other kinds that are less obvious, too. For example, you might ruminate, where you focus, to an extreme extent, on your depressive symptoms and on the implications of these. For example, if you feel sad or upset about something, you might hyperfocus on that feeling of sadness instead of trying to process it and change to a more positive emotion once that initial emotion is processed. You might have done this yourself, thinking about a situation over and over again, making yourself feel sadder and sadder, and getting so deep into your overthinking that you end up confused between what the facts are, and how you are feeling.

Another common mechanism is emotional numbing, and it is the opposite of ruminating. Instead of being overwhelmed by your feelings, you choose to completely shut them down. This way, you are relieving yourself from the stress and anxiety that come with the situation you are in, but you are not actually processing those emotions. Feeling stressed, anxious, angry or sad about a situation is normal. It's part of the human experience to live through all these emotions and feelings! It's important to accept that this is the case, because otherwise, you only bottle up emotions endlessly without ever emptying the bottle. This doesn't just affect you, it also affects your partner, who may feel like you aren't telling them the full story, or like you aren't sharing your emotions with them. This can make them feel uneasy, or like a big blow-up is about to happen once all the emotions crash down on you at once.

You may have also tried to escape a situation before to avoid it altogether and to avoid difficult feelings. When something stresses us out, and when we feel like we aren't able to cope at all, we just try to escape that situation. We run away from it. We avoid facing it altogether to make sure that we never have to face it again. But of course, this doesn't always work. Similarly, we might daydream, which is where you can stop living in reality and imagine a better one instead. Of course, we all daydream once in a while. We're bored at work and we think about going on a trip elsewhere to escape our desk job. These are normal kinds of daydreaming, but if you find yourself spending hours daydreaming about being in a different place or situation, that changes things. This may be a coping mechanism you are using to escape the reality, or to feel like you have control over your ability to exit the situation.

Anxious avoidance is similar to the former, but different in that you actively avoid situations that could make you upset. You will actively avoid events that you feel may make you react negatively, or may make you feel a certain way. You might be fearful of losing your partner, so you choose to simply avoid talking to them about what's stressing you out because you fear they may react badly. You may avoid all kinds of conflicts with them because of this stress that you won't overcome.

Stress can make us all feel like we aren't in control, and it can make us do many things that we may end up regretting. It can also make us feel like we don't know how to handle a certain situation, and that can be quite scary, especially if you have an anxious or avoidant attachment style! But using maladaptive coping mechanisms won't help this, and it is much more likely to lead to the degradation of your relationship. It hurts your communication, and it can make your partner feel like you aren't willing to make your relationship work by working on it together, as a team.

Trust and Intimacy

Your attachment style will of course greatly influence how and whether you feel comfortable with trust and intimacy. After all, when we are securely attached to someone else, it is much less likely that we feel insecure in the relationship overall. Instead, chances are that we fully trust our partners because we have no reason not to. If they haven't given us any reason to feel worried about their actions or what they might do, then why worry?

Well, to those of you who are anxiously attached or avoidant, the picture looks a lot different. You might feel like being intimate is something you do not struggle with at all because you always feel like it is a moment where you are the closest to them. You might feel closer to them after intimacy, and it feels great. Trust-wise, it gets a little bit tricky. You might trust them and truly believe that they are honest and trustworthy, but your anxious style may make you struggle to follow through with that trust. You might feel like, although they don't give you any reasons to doubt them, you still aren't convinced, and there isn't much that they could do to convince you, indeed.

For avoidants, however, that might actually sound horrendous, vulnerability? Voluntarily? You might feel like you don't want to be intimate because this shows vulnerability. And remember! Being intimate does not equate to sexuality! You can be intimate emotionally, where you share your ideas, thoughts, and emotions with someone else. The same is true for the trust aspect, you probably struggle to trust the person because you have been burned in the past, so you prefer protecting yourself as much as you can.

Personal Growth and Relationship Evolution

The final element we are considering here is your personal growth (both partners) and the evolution of your relationship. A relationship isn't meant to be stagnant. Yes, it is meant to be comfortable and to feel good, but that should not mean that it is getting stagnant. Instead, it is meant to be something in which both of you can grow! You are in this relationship because it adds to your life, not because it takes away from it. Therefore, you personally should grow, and you should grow as a couple, too.

Again, how easy this is depends on the kind of attachment you have. If you have a secure attachment, chances are that both you and your partner are all about growth and developing new aspects of yourself. You want each other to become the best versions of yourself, and you feel secure in knowing that this is possible without the relationship ending. Or, you are secure in the fact that if the relationship ends because of this growth, that does not mean that the relationship is a failure, quite the opposite. Instead, it means that you were secure enough in yourself to know that it is better for both you and your partner to separate to continue growing as part of your lives, instead of thinking of staying in this relationship, letting it make both of you stagnant, and then turning to resentment when you both feel like you have missed out on good growth opportunities.

For anxious people, this is different, of course. With an insecure attachment, changes and personal growth can make you feel like you are potentially going to change the relationship as a whole. Changing and becoming someone different because of growth might be terrifying, what if your partnership no longer works as a result of this change? What if you aren't the amazing match you were when you once met one another? Likewise, you might worry if your relationship is changing, new jobs, new location, new friends, etc. Or, you might actually hinder your own growth by focusing too much on the anxiety you feel around your relationship.

Avoidants, I haven't forgotten about you. Unlike those who are anxious, you may avoid emotional connection. You may not be able to grow your relationship and develop it further because you may feel more comfortable putting some emotional distance between the two of you, since it feels more comfortable to have control over how much you attach yourself to someone. This can stop your growth as well, because focusing on protecting yourself and your heart can take precedence over other aspects of your life, and you might miss out on fun opportunities to do great things that push you further in life.

As a couple, and as individuals, you both need to be able to adapt to life changes, especially if you are in this relationship for the long run. A securely attached couple can do this well, they use each other as an anchor so they can handle life transitions together, and they feel safe and able to confront their issues if they do end up dealing with some. This looks much different for people who are insecure in the relationship, whether they are avoidant or anxious. The more stress there is in the relationship, the more the person may struggle to feel like the relationship is worth it. You may feel like with extra stress, you cannot cope, and you may turn to self-sabotage to prevent more hurt and pain. Ultimately, your relationship can go in flames because of this.

Having explored what attachment styles are, how they work, and how they impact your relationship, it's time to look at something different, how they are formed. Why? Because this will give us loads of insights into why you may have the style you have, and hence, why you may be struggling with overthinking. Remember that your attachment style is not something you are "stuck" with. It's very much something that you can change and impact positively, and that starts with understanding why you are attached the way you are, and what you can do about it. Let's have a look.

Chapter Three

The Formation of Attachment Styles

While reading the first few chapters of this book, you might have felt like you resonated more or less with one or another attachment style. I will go out on a limb here and suggest that if you are still reading this book, you have an insecure attachment style, which is making you want to learn more about what you can do about it to change things. To change things, we need to understand how they originated. So, throughout this chapter, we will explore one by one the elements that lead to the formation of a certain attachment style over another, helping you pinpoint why you may have developed an anxious, avoidant, or disorganized style. We have already explored a few reasons briefly, trauma, parents' relationships... but there are many more that you may be surprised to read about.

Romantic Relationships

Let's start with the obvious ones, your romantic relationships. Chances are that if you are reading this book, you have been involved in a few semi-serious or fully serious relationships. These relationships may have been very successful, somewhat successful with their occasional ups and downs, or entirely unsuccessful, and you probably have an idea of the reason why they turned out the way they did. Perhaps you loved your partner deeply but weren't able to show this to them because you were worried about them hurting you. You may have also had a hard time sharing your feelings because you felt like this would be vulnerable, and you did not feel comfortable with this.

You may have been told by partners in the past that you should "open up more" or "feel comfortable sharing how you are feeling," and although you understood, you couldn't understand how to do so without feeling so uncomfortable. To you, it may have felt like you were sharing parts of yourself and your personality that you simply didn't feel comfortable sharing with others, either because they could hurt you, because they could abandon you, or because opening yourself up to that extent carried too many other risks. This is typical of the avoidant style.

On the other hand, your stress and anxieties surrounding relationships may have been the cause of your problems. For example, although you felt like the highs were very high, when you felt slightly insecure about your partner or your relationship, that anxiety may have held you back from being all-in. It may have made you feel like you needed to cling onto them, or like you had to constantly ask for their reassurance to feel secure in that relationship. You may have felt like no matter how many times your partner told you that they loved you and cared for you, you never truly believed it or felt that you needed just a bit more reassurance. These kinds of behaviors can become tiring and overwhelming for a partner who may get the feeling that nothing they do is enough, and that they need to continuously reaffirm their love for you in order to be believed. As a person with an anxious attachment style, your need for reassurance and validation may have been the cause of the disintegration of your relationships.

Maybe you are reading this thinking, "well, it's a bit of both!" And that's typically what we expect from a disorganized attachment style. Sometimes, you feel anxious about the relationship, and that may make you adopt behaviors typically associated with an avoidant style. You have reassurance, you feel loved, and you feel less anxious when you are shown this by your partner, but then, you may feel overwhelmed by that love and distance yourself. This is inconsistent and hard to predict, and it may have become too much for a partner.

This isn't to say that you and your behavior are the reason for relationships not working, but rather that your attachment style, and therefore the behavior that results from this, may have played a role in this. Specifically, your relationships reinforce your existing attachment styles.

Reinforcing Attachment Styles

How? Let's explore that. First, your romantic relationships are full of interactions with partners that will either confirm or challenge your expectations when it comes to closeness, whether you can rely on someone, whether you can be emotionally safe around them, and so on. For example, if you have primarily found yourself in relationships where you rarely felt safe, where the person treated you poorly, where they disrespected you or made you feel like you could not rely on them for love and support, you are more likely to find yourself increasingly anxious in the future. You might find a fantastic new partner, but the behavior you have experienced may make you feel like everybody acts this way, and like you will never be able to find a partner who is kind and loving to you.

Similarly, as we know, those with an avoidant attachment style will tend to feel safer the more they protect themselves from others by distancing themselves from others. Well, this may have led you to have relationships in which you could never truly open yourself up, or where you struggled to express your emotions. To a secure person, or worse, an anxious person, this may have been a deal breaker as they may have expected that their partner would share their feelings and emotions much openly, and they may have felt like they could not connect to you. So, by overthinking and fearing openness, your relationships ended up with heartbreak and most likely a reinforcement of your attachment style, because you may have felt abandoned.

The relationship itself can reinforce patterns of anxious attachment too, because if one is constantly met with dismissiveness, one may simply have the anxiety reinforced, which creates a cycle where one is needier and needier, and more and more insecure. The same is true for avoidant styles, the more you are told to open up and share your feelings, the more you might feel insecure about it, and the more you may want to retract and distance yourself from that request. Or, you might even look for a partner who honors your need for more privacy, which helps you avoid having to address the avoidance of intimacy and emotional expression.

Negative Past Experiences

Of course, your negative relationship experiences will also impact you. Although you may have previously been a securely attached person, going through a negative experience such as being betrayed, or dealing with a relationship with someone who was inconsistent, can worsen your attachment style and/or change it entirely. It can make it difficult for you to trust people again, making you more avoidant, or can make you anxious and in need of more reassurance. It could also make you adopt a more disorganized attachment style, because although you feel anxious at times, at other times, such as when you are reminded of your past experiences or emotional times in your past, you feel like pulling back because you are worried of getting hurt again. These negative relationship experiences might have reinforced the insecurities you had, or even created new ones! and that's tough to deal with.

Your romantic relationships will also form how you get attached depending on the experiences you have had with long-term commitment and intimacy. For example, if your experiences are mainly negative, you might struggle to commit in the long-term. You might feel like long-term commitment is equivalent to being jailed by a relationship, especially if you tend to be in the avoidant style. Intimacy, as discussed earlier, might also be something you avoid to stay away from all chances of getting hurt. For anxious individuals, it's the opposite, commitment might be great because it shows security, and intimacy is a way to feel close.

Friendships and Peer Relationships

Although we focus a lot on our romantic relationships, we should pay better attention to our friendships and peer relationships, because of the power that they hold over us! The friends we have are the ones who are there for us whenever we feel down or we struggle. They are the ones here or us when we don't know what to do next. They are the ones who watch us grow and become better people! So, they play a significant role in our attachment style.

For example, they have great influence over our social development and attachment in general. Think about it this way: the friendships you build and the interactions you have with your peers as a child have partly shaped who you are today. They contribute to your socialization, which is where we start forming attachments with people. This is when we learn how we can trust other people and who we are as part of a member in society. It's how we learn how to be sociable beings, and our friends play a great role in this.

For example, we learn how we like to be treated through our friends, because we learn what feels good and what doesn't. We also learn how to set boundaries through our friends, because we learn that there are certain behaviors that we are okay with, and others that we are not okay with.

Learning Emotional Regulation

Not only this, but we also learn a lot about how to manage our emotions, conflicts, and different views on things. Life would be boring if we all had the same opinions and ways of viewing things, and this is why we are confronted with different views. As we grow up surrounded by children, we learn how to manage our emotions. We are taught by adults how to deal with our emotions, when we are angry, sad, or frustrated, we use words instead of hitting. We don't yell, we speak with the right tone of voice. These weren't magically acquired, we learn them by being social with other human beings. We learn that there are behaviors that are acceptable generally-speaking, and others that are unacceptable.

We also observe other people, so we learn how our actions affect others. For example, we learn that if we yell at people, they are less likely to want to communicate with us. If we talk to people with respect, however, we get more from the conversation. We also learn that saying certain things to people makes them upset, so we learn through these social experiences that some things are right and others are wrong. This socialization is important to the kind of attachment style we have. For example, it might affect whether you feel like you can trust people. Or, if you grew up in an environment that did not teach you the concept of boundaries or saying no, you may have realized as an adult that you struggle to set them because you don't know how, or you worry that doing so might lead other people to react negatively (depending on how your household was like, primarily).

Just like your romantic relationships, your friendships and peer relationships also reinforce or even modify the attachment style you might have. Friendships that are positive and which add to your life are usually characterized by friends who are reliable, trustworthy, and who show you respect (and vice versa!). The kind of friends you have impacts your view of what the right kind of treatment is. For example, if you have friends who don't tend to treat you super well, whether that's by talking to you disrespectfully or leaving you hanging, you are likely to have this idea that this is a "normal" kind of behavior, and not the kind of behavior that you deserve. You might internalize the idea that this is not wrong in any way, shape, or form, which then makes it more likely for you to end up in a romantic relationship with someone who treats you like this too.

Positive Influences That Act as a Sounding Board

But of course, your friends have the potential to do great things for you as well! Great friends can help boost your confidence and make you question whether you are thinking rationally or not when you are anxious. They can help you think through your relationships, and they can act as a sounding board when you aren't sure of whether something is right or wrong. For example, if you have an insecure attachment style, having a friend with a secure one can be great to have the right examples and to have someone to ask questions to when you aren't sure of something. They can tell you what kind of behavior they feel is right and they can discuss your point of view and perspective when you feel like you aren't sure of yourself. These friends also teach you about the kind of loyalty and reliability to expect from people, and they can tell you when they feel like the person you are with isn't being loyal enough.

Unfortunately, since friendships and peers play such an important role in our childhood and in who we become, this also means that they can have a negative impact. If you have been bullied, or if you were rejected as a child by friends, you may have developed feelings of insecurity, or even worthlessness. This naturally can translate into your adult life too, where you need to be reassured by your partner to feel like you are wanted and loved. The rejection could also lead to a more avoidant kind of behavior as you try to protect yourself from feeling the same things you felt when you were younger.

Finally, here's an important one: self-concept. It's an important idea in psychology. Your self-concept is similar to your identity, or how you view yourself. It develops throughout the years, and it is greatly influenced by your friends. Your self-concept is essentially the collection of beliefs about yourself, who you are, what you are, how you think, what you offer to people, your value, how you think others see you, and so on. This self-concept is influenced by your friends who give you feedback. You were maybe known as the clown of the classroom, as the very nice girl who always helped people in math class, or as the theater kid. These identifications are part of your self-concept, and they're reinforced by your friends. This self-concept can be negative or positive, and it affects the attachment behaviors and expectations you have in these relationships. As a result, this transfers onto your adult relationships too.

Parenting and Family Dynamics

Last but certainly not least, we have to consider the parenting style and family dynamics in which you grew up. We have seen briefly how our upbringing, specifically our parents, can influence the kind of partner we are. For example, a parent who was absent may lead to an avoidant style, while an abusive parent or a parent who made their child work hard for their love may lead a person to have an anxious attachment style.

We All Need to Feel Safe

First things first, as a child, your need is to have a grown up, regardless of whether that's a parent or a guardian, whom you trust. This person, to your very young eyes, is someone that you view as being a survival resource. Without them, you would die. So, naturally, this is an extremely strong bond, an important one, and one that will affect you for the rest of your life. Whether you feel safe or not, whether you feel like this bond is here to protect you or not, and whether you feel like you are unconditionally loved by this person, can make a crucial difference in your attachment styles later on. When this need isn't fulfilled, such as when your parent is neglectful and/or makes you feel like you need to act a certain way to earn love, this can lead to an insecure attachment style. The quality of the care you receive, and importantly, the responsiveness as well as the availability of your caregiver directly influences how your attachment style develops.

How does this look for a secure parent-child attachment style? It is characterized by the parent showing consistent sensitivity and responsiveness to the child's needs. So, if the child is crying out, is seeking attention, or requires responsiveness, a parenting style that would lead to a secure attachment would respond to this promptly and consistently. This way, the child feels that they can trust the person caring for them. They feel safe. Importantly, they feel a positive sense of self because the person caring for them, which also is the most important person in that child's life at the time, shows that they will always respond to their needs, no matter what they may be.

When it comes to insecure attachment styles, the picture looks a bit different. For anxious attachments, the parent may give inconsistent caregiving. For example, the child might be uncertain of whether they will receive love and attention, whether they will be cared for, whether their parent will respond to their needs, and therefore, this translates into an anxious attachment style later in life. On the other hand, if the parent is mainly unavailable or rejects the child's calls for responses and does not give them the care they need, the child has to be self-reliant. They also learn through this kind of behavior that emotional closeness is dismissed, and that this is the right way to act when others try to get close to them. In the disorganized style, we see a mix of both. For example, we might see this in children who experienced childhood traumas, such as being raised by a narcissistic parent who only gave out love sometimes, and who abandoned or refused to care for the needs of the child unless conditions were met, or randomly, depending on their mood.

Intergenerational Transmission

Your attachment style may have also been transmitted from your parents down to you. That's right, intergenerational transmission of attachment patterns plays a big role in this. Your parents were most likely unaware of this but unconsciously modeled the attachment behaviors that they experienced when they were children. For example, if they were raised in an environment where emotions were looked down upon and crying was discouraged, they may have transferred this to you. If they were raised in a household where praise and responsiveness to needs was earned and not simply given as needed, they may pass this on to you as well. Can you break the cycle? Of course. By reading this very book, you're completing the first step to this: becoming aware of your patterns. Healing is the next step, and it's something we will be moving on to shortly.

But before we start the healing process, let's look at some ways in which your upbringing might have affected who you are, how you act in relationships, and how you overthink. As you can imagine, the kind of parenting style and therefore the attachment style you develop will have influenced your emotional and social development. As mentioned earlier in the section on friendships, your attachment style affects how you can regulate your emotions, your self-esteem, and whether you can form healthy relationships with both friends and adults outside your family. But on top of this, your cognitive development is influenced by your attachment style. A secure attachment is linked with much better cognitive outcomes, namely because as a child, you feel safe to explore and to learn from your environment. On the other hand, if you have an insecure attachment, you may have been less comfortable exploring new things and learning.

Your resilience may have also been affected by your upbringing, as research has shown that children who are securely attached are, generally-speaking, a lot more resilient whenever they're dealing with challenges. On the other hand, if you have an insecure attachment style, you may be more vulnerable when stressful situations arise.

Now that we know more about how specifically our attachment styles form, it's time to start looking more specifically at what we are fixing. This book, after all, is about helping you overcome your overthinking patterns, many of which are likely at the root of the problems you have been experiencing in your relationship. Whether you are an anxious person or have an avoidant attachment style, start believing that these problems can be addressed and that you can get to a secure attachment style. We've seen in quite a lot of detail how these attachment styles are not innate, which is great news as it means that they can be changed.

Chapter Four

Challenges and Pitfalls in Relationships

It's time to start applying the concept of attachment styles more specifically to the challenges we see in many relationships. Whether you are dealing with relationship insecurity, have trust issues or jealousy, or are struggling with separation anxiety or fear of abandonment, there are ways to confront those feelings and to make changes so you feel more secure in your relationship. Of course, this is not a one-size-fits-all, but it is a good place to start to feel more secure with your partner and to slowly halt your overthinking.

Dynamics of Anxious-Avoidant Relationships

Let's start by considering what an anxious relationship, or an avoidant relationship, may look like. Starting with an anxious attachment in a relationship, as we have seen, if you are someone with a lot of anxiety around relationships, you may be looking for a lot of reassurance and validation from your partner. You may fear that you will be abandoned and/or rejected by them, so you may need a lot of reassurance here and there that things are going well. However, if you need more than just the occasional "I love you" or reassuring sentence, and if you feel like this is something that you need on a constant basis, so much so that your partner seems to be tired of it, you may be the anxious partner in the relationship.

Likewise, you might be sensitive to your partner's behavior. You might pay attention to how they react, to their moods, to how available they are, to their actions, and so on. You might feel like these factors represent how stable your relationship is, but this is a wrong approach. This person is only one of the partners in the relationship, so their mood or actions cannot be the sole determinant of the entire relationship and whether it is working or not.

You might also have highs and lows, or be emotionally volatile. This might depend on how close or far you feel from your partner (both actually and literally speaking). This might make you feel like you are constantly either very happy or very sad and depressed, and you may also feel emotionally exhausted from adapting your emotional response and reaction to your partner's moods and actions.

Your partner also experiences the result of this anxiety. They may feel like their way of showing you their affection and love is never enough because you are constantly asking for more reassurance. They may feel like they need to watch out for how they speak, what they do, when they are available, and so on, to make sure that you don't feel abandoned or left aside. You may not know it, but to them, it can feel like they're constantly working hard to avoid making you feel like you aren't loved or appreciated.

Moving onto the avoidant attachment style, the dynamics differ greatly. There is usually a common pattern, namely the pursuer-distancer pattern. As an avoidant partner, you might be in this dynamic if your partner, who needs closeness, triggers your own need for distance, and vice versa. So, you both end up in a situation where you are frustrated and dissatisfied. Communication, which would be ideal in this case, is unfortunately also a problem in this setting because you have contrasting needs and coping mechanisms, especially if your partner is anxious.

You might feel like you are overwhelmed by the conflict, while your partner might not feel heard, which is a recipe for failure. You might be speaking to one another, but you aren't truly listening. This kind of relationship is also one that reinforces the behaviors. This is especially in the case where an anxious person is with an avoidant person, which occurs often. The anxious partner might become a lot more worried about being abandoned, while the avoidant partner might feel like their independence is threatened. Even with a secure partner, the avoidant might struggle to fulfill their partner's needs of openness and vulnerability.

So, what's the outcome? Well, you are emotionally disconnected, and you struggle to overcome conflict and come to resolutions. Without the ability to communicate, and without feeling like your needs are met if you are an anxious partner, you feel emotionally disconnected from your partner and you feel that they aren't responding to the needs you are saying you need them to meet. You and/or your partner might feel lonely in this relationship because although you are together, you aren't on the same page at all. Instead, you are focusing on what you are missing from the relationship, and neither person is happy!

Overcoming Relationship Insecurity

One of the biggest concerns my clients come to me with is insecurities surrounding their relationship. They may not know why, they may not know what needs to change, but they feel insecure in this relationship. Perhaps they feel like their partner is going to leave them, or like they are going to start loving someone else. They might otherwise feel like they have no independence, or like their partner is asking them intrusive questions, guess which one is which! Insecurity can create a pattern of thinking in which you lose yourself.

You ask yourself questions, and the more you think, the more you lose yourself in those thoughts and start thinking about what you are thinking instead of what is actually happening. You might feel like you are getting lost in your own thoughts, what really is happening, and how much of the emotions you are having are actually rooted in anxiety over reality? It gets confusing, but the more you think, the more worried you get, and the more anxious you become. This creates a vicious cycle, you can't stop feeling anxious, and it's taking a serious toll on you, stopping you from working, studying, or whatever else you are doing, and you feel like you can't remember what exactly it is that's making you anxious. It's not a fun place to be in. It's an even less fun feeling to deal with. So, let's overcome that.

Where is it coming from?

Like we did so for your attachment style, to understand what the problem is and how to fix it, we need to identify its source. So, we are going to start by looking at

78

the roots of your insecurities. Think back to the previous chapter, and think about the parts that resonated with you more than others. Do you feel like your upbringing could have led you to feeling this way? Or, could it be the previous relationships you have had that led you here? If you have ever dealt with betrayal, or if you had childhood attachment issues, try to clarify what they were. You might just have found the reason why you might feel insecure in your relationships.

Next, look for triggering situations. These "triggers" are just situations or behaviors that make you feel insecure. Think about the moments where you feel the most insecure, or where you feel the least secure in your relationship. Does it have to do with communication? Is it when you see that your partner's communication patterns seem to be changing? Does it have to do with the way they talk to you? Their mood? Do you feel triggered when they seem less interested in hanging out with you than they are interested in seeing their friends? Pinpoint that trigger. Once you know what it is, it becomes a lot easier to manage your emotions when this happens, because you know the reason why you are feeling the way you feel.

Next, we need to have a look at your self-esteem. Many times, insecurity emerges as a result of low self-esteem. As an anxiously attached person, you may feel like you are not worthy of people's love. You may feel like the other person is with you out of pure chance, and therefore, that you need to earn their love, remember, this is a key component of childhood attachment development. You may feel like you aren't good enough for others, like there are better options, or like you are never going to be able to give your partner enough.

So, you are anxious. You're worried that they are only a few days away from ending things. They've had a bad day and they're tired? No, their mood isn't because of their 12-hour shift; to you, it feels like it's because they are no longer interested in a relationship with you. Or, you feel like they are less available at the moment, often asking if you can stay in instead of going on dates? Could it be that big project that has them staying up until midnight three times a week? Of course, but to your anxious mind, it's your fault. It has to be something that is related to you. You catch the drift?

To the avoidants among us, it's no easier. On your end, you may be avoiding big conversations and may feel like you are being pushed into a box whenever your partner asks you to be a bit more open with your feelings, to plan something more extensively, or to commit to some sort of long term relationship. You might also feel defensive if they show the slightest sign of wanting to intrude on your protective barrier. You might feel triggered by them telling you that they want more from you, or that they feel like they aren't emotionally connected to you enough.

They might need you to go the extra mile so they feel safer in the relationship, but that might simply not be something that you are comfortable with. So, you feel insecure, in part because you might not feel like you are enough, but also in part because you might not feel like the person in front of you understands you. You feel like they are pushing you too much, pushing you to keep doing things that you don't feel comfortable with, things you just don't want to do. It's a difficult spot to be in, and it's normal that you don't feel entirely secure. So, try to identify which part of these situations is triggering to you. Then, once we've done this, we can start working on your self-esteem.

The self-esteem starts with being kind to yourself. I know, I know… How cliche. And yet, it is something you keep hearing because it is true.

How can you expect to have self-esteem if you are not kind to yourself, compassionate, and welcoming of your own mistakes? We all make them, and although it's indeed a good idea to make sure to learn from them, this doesn't mean that you should be extremely harsh on yourself.

Think of it this way: I am doing my best with what I have. If you have made mistakes in the past, and if you are ashamed of them, start by being apologetic to yourself. Forgive yourself. Accept that it's okay to make mistakes, and that you can move on. This will help you build a more positive view of yourself, instead of focusing on the "bad" parts or something that makes you less of a person. Try it now. Think of something you blame yourself a lot for, and instead of being mean or harsh to yourself, accept that you made a mistake. Then, choose to move on and not to go back to this mistake to then blame yourself again.

Part of growing your self-esteem also includes working on your growth as a person. You are someone with a tremendous amount of talent. You are capable of doing great things. We all have talents and capabilities, so it is something that we truly can all do! What's even more important in all this is that by working on your self-growth, you have more time to think about your personal interests and what you care about instead of focusing on the other person in the partnership. Instead of placing most of your energy on understanding your partner, on gauging how they feel, or on avoiding harsh conversations to protect yourself, you are working on yourself and growing as a person.

Developing new skills, becoming an expert at something, or just dedicating some time to something that you care a lot about is a great way to focus on yourself and your growth, and this undoubtedly brings you a feeling of accomplishment. It brings you the feeling of being focused on yourself and becoming a better person, which can be freeing, especially if you currently spend a lot of time thinking about your relationship or your partner!

Are you communicating well?

The dreaded communication question. By now, it is pretty clear that communicating well is extremely important for a relationship to actually work. Without this communication, you cannot share your points of view, how you feel about one another, and what you are worried or concerned about without the entire conversation blowing up into a conflict. Not only this, but without communication, you end up potentially making decisions based on assumptions, instead of making them based on the information that you have received and that you are sure of. Communication is a non-negotiable.

But what does that mean? It's more than just the words you say. You need to express your needs and your fears. Now, dear avoidants, relax. This is something you can prepare yourself for. You can practice, and you can decide to start small. Instead of plunging into an ice cold water, you can start by focusing on what you find most important. Tell your partner that you don't feel comfortable talking about this, so that you need them to be empathetic and to listen closely so you can feel heard.

To those listening to their partner speaking, remember that listening is just as important as actually speaking. If your partner wants to speak to you about some concerns they are having, it's time to listen to them. It's time to think about what they are telling you, and to truly listen to what they are saying before you jump and respond right away. This is when you need to put aside your need to respond, especially if you tend to feel attacked during conflicts, and when you need to think about what the person is sharing with you.

With communication comes trust. If you have identified that trust is something that is lacking in your relationship, or at least on your side, try to pinpoint why this is the case. Have you had experiences where your partner made you feel like they couldn't be trusted? How much of this is applicable to this new partner? Ask yourself if the person has shown consistency in their actions and behaviors before. Have they been shown to be untrustworthy or dishonest? If not, what makes you feel like this is going to happen, and where is that fear coming from? Can you rationalize this feeling, or do you have a truly well-founded reason for it? Regardless of the reason, if you want this relationship to work, trust is a must. If you cannot trust, the relationship will not survive the challenges it will face throughout the future.

Are you open to being intimate?

Remember, intimacy does not equate to sexuality. We are intimate in many ways, and some would even say that emotional intimacy is a special kind of intimacy! Are you able to share your vulnerabilities? If not, again, try to pinpoint why. Do you feel unsafe with your partner? Do you feel like they are not giving you the space to be intimate? Or, is it entirely unrelated to them? You can work on having safe boundaries that both respect you and your comfort zone, but that also respect what your partner needs from you to feel emotionally connected. If this is something you struggle to agree on, it may be time to work with a couples therapist, as having a third party involved and helping you figure things out can be very comforting!

Addressing Trust Issues and Jealousy

Let's look at trust and jealousy as two important elements that could affect your relationship's viability. As an overthinker, chances are that you also tend to feel jealous, or that you lack trust. You may feel like although you want to trust your partner, you have been too hurt in the past, you have been betrayed, or it is not them you don't trust, but other people around them. This lack of trust, which will often fuel an anxious attachment style, can slowly eat away at your relationship. If your partner constantly feels like they are not proving their love for you enough, or feel like you think that they are cheating, it can be difficult for them to deal with this. They love you, and they want what's best for you. So, of course, being accused of cheating, or not being trusted, can be difficult to accept.

Your trust issues and/or jealousy can be addressed, and we are starting the same way as above. Start by looking inside and find the source of that lack of trust. Have you been severely hurt before, and now, you have a hard time trusting others? Do you have personal insecurities that are holding you back from trusting this partner? Were you raised in a family where you didn't feel you could trust people? Your trust issues might be from the relationship itself, you might have caught them lying, for example.

Then, again, look at the triggers. What makes you jealous? What makes you feel like you cannot trust the person? What is the trigger that makes it happen? Are you unable to trust them because you feel like every time you do so, you get hurt again? It's important not to associate a previous relationship's events to the new relationship, even if it feels like it gives you a bit of control because it makes you feel like you are preparing yourself for the potentiality of getting hurt.

It might feel unintuitive, but speak to your partner about these feelings too. Don't accuse them, but explain to them how you feel. If the source of this lack of trust is in yourself, as in, if you know that they are trustworthy but you need to be better at avoiding overthinking and at trusting them instead, share this with them.

Your partner should be consistent with their behavior, and they should be transparent with their actions. This is how you can truly trust them. Otherwise, it keeps you on the tip of your toes until you can better understand what their pattern is, only for them to change it all over again! And if the trust has been broken and you do want to rebuild it, give yourself time. It's a process that won't take place overnight. It requires you to show patience, to make an effort, to forgive, and to accept that you are now moving on. Set new boundaries to help you protect yourself and your heart, and look for some help from a therapist if you feel that your efforts together are not having enough of an effect!

Help! I Have Separation Anxiety and Fear Being Abandoned

As humans, it is in our nature to want to be loved, and to want people to want us. It is in our nature to fear being abandoned or left behind, because this puts us at risk. Or, at least, it used to. Sure, being abandoned or rejected might no longer mean imminent death because we don't have a community watching over us as we sleep, but it is still something that is deeply ingrained in us as something that we want to avoid at all costs. It doesn't feel good to be unwanted.

And yet, unfortunately, there are certain things that we simply cannot control. One of these is ensuring that the person we love and share a life or relationship with stays with us forever. We might want to have that safety, and we might want to feel like we retain that control over someone, but in reality, we can never control what someone else does. All we can do is hope that we both remain happy and fulfilled with that relationship.

Nevertheless, this doesn't take away from the fact that being anxious of being rejected or abandoned sucks. It's hard to deal with that feeling. We feel like something is wrong, like something bad's about to happen, and our anxious brains convince us that this is it, the breakup is imminent! Of course, it isn't that simple. But again, to get past that anxiety, you first need to know where it stems from. You need to reflect on the kinds of experiences you might have had in the past, and think about how they might have made you so fearful or anxious. Think of your childhood experiences, could they be the problem? Now, think of your past relationship traumas, could that be the reason?

Next, you will want to acknowledge the impact that this has on you. It's hard! But, it's needed. This event, this situation, has had an impact so great on you that you feel anxious if your partner chooses to leave. It's normal to worry about the relationship ending once in a while; for example, while they are traveling abroad and you remain back home. You might get worried then or in other similar instances because the circumstances are completely different. But spending each day of this relationship worried about your relationship ending isn't healthy, and, it's quite sad, as you are missing out on a great time with your partner!

Think, as you did above, of the triggers for these feelings. What makes you feel this way about your relationship? What does your partner do, or what has to happen for you to feel insecure like this relationship is about to end? Are there specific situations, behaviors, emotions, etc that make you feel more anxious or fearful than others?

Now, when those moments arise, I want you to take a moment to breathe in deeply and to practice mindfulness. Think about how you feel at that very moment. Focus on the emotions you are feeling, and let yourself feel them. Take some time to relax, to compose your thoughts, and to pay attention to exactly how you felt when this happened. This is to help you become more self-aware of how you feel when the triggers happen. Unfortunately, triggers can make it very difficult to focus on anything other than the anger we have, or the anxiety, so much so that we forget to try to process why it's there. So, be mindful when these triggers come up.

This is where it gets hard. You will have to confront your codependency tendencies, if you have them. Codependency happens when you have low self-esteem and desperately need someone's approval. The result? You have an unhealthy attachment to this person, and you start putting this person's needs right in front of your own. Additionally, as Dr. Exelberg, a licensed psychologist and author, says, "Codependency is a circular relationship in which one person needs the other person, who in turn, needs to be needed. The codependent person, known as 'the giver,' feels worthless unless they are needed by and making sacrifices for the enabler, otherwise known as 'the taker." In other words, to get past your codependency, if you indeed have this tendency, you will need to confront your need to feel needed.

It's tough! When we feel needed, we feel secure. We feel like as long as we can give this other person something that they want or need, that we are securing our spot in their lives. This is a false idea, and it is a way for toxic individuals to make their way through our lives by exploiting our need to feel needed. So, you need to return to yourself. To focus on yourself. You need to focus on what you are interested in, what you want to do, what you want to become, skills you want to learn, and so on. You need to focus on yourself, instead of on making someone else happy, and no, it won't be easy!

Part of focusing on yourself also involves building a strong support network. And before you think it, yes, your partner is part of that network, but only part of it. They shouldn't be the only person in that network. It's a network, it's full of people who are there for you when you need it. This means that you need more than just one person, and that you should welcome having all kinds of people in that network, ready to help you when you need it. You should have people that you can speak to when you feel like you are overthinking. These are the people who are there for you, to talk when you need to, and to listen to you so they can help by giving you their perspective. For example, if you end up feeling super anxious about something that has happened in your relationship, or if you simply need to speak to someone about how anxious you are feeling, you need a support network that you can turn to. These are the people who can help you break down the events, ask you questions, and help you make sense of it all. They give you emotional security and help you avoid being overly reliant on your partner. As a result, if you end up feeling like you need reassurance from your partner but also feel like this is coming from a place of anxiety, you can ask your friends and other people in your network to help you break that down so you can understand where it's coming from.

Focus on Self-Care

Now, there are more "cliché" aspects to this too, like taking care of yourself physically and emotionally. Look, I understand that you may not enjoy exercise, or that it may be the last thing on your mind when you feel anxious and like you just need to get out of your head. But physical activity and self-care in general are not only things we turn to when we need to feel less anxious, they are there as preventative methods too. Research shows that physical activity boosts our self-esteem, our mood, and even our energy. It also shows that it reduces our stress, our likelihood of developing dementia, and many other conditions. Evidence shows that "the greatest improvements in health status are seen when people who are least fit become physically active," which shows that if you aren't currently active, this may be where you can start to see some changes in how you feel. Separation anxiety is a form of stress, and keeping yourself busy by exercising, as well as the overall stress-reducing benefits, is important.

That goes beyond the health aspect as well. Physical activity is part of taking good care of yourself. Think of it this way: on days when you don't shower, don't eat well, haven't slept enough, and don't move much, how do you feel? Do you feel like you have it all together, or do you feel poorly? Do you have high self-esteem, or do you feel badly about yourself? There is value in taking care of ourselves, our bodies, and our minds, because it makes us feel good about ourselves. It makes us feel like we are taking care of ourselves. When you feel anxious, especially if it is separation anxiety, take yourself out to lunch, go for a long walk in the sun, do something that makes you feel good. Take care of yourself in ways that you know make you feel good, and focus on yourself instead of your partner. This is for your emotional health too! When you are in a good mindspace, take some time to think of activities that make you feel good. Then, keep this list close by for times when you need that moment of self-care.

Therapy Work

Although taking care of yourself through self-care is a great way to address the symptoms of separation anxiety, you will also greatly benefit from working on yourself and your anxiety as a whole by reaching out to professionals to get the help you need. Therapy is a great way to get this kind of support, as it can give you the strategies to cope with your feelings. Not only this, but it can help you uncover the reasons why you might be feeling this way, helping you get past these feelings so you can develop a more secure attachment style. For example, it can help you understand why you feel anxious, get to the bottom of the triggers that make you feel this way, and give you strategies to overcome both the feelings and the reasons that cause these.

Therapy can also be done as a couple, where you can grow more trustworthy of one another. It's a great way for you and your partner to look into what makes you feel anxious and overthink, and to help them understand where this may be coming from. It can help you gain a better understanding of those feelings so you know how to best support each other, while giving you a "middle man" to help you navigate conversations that can be quite difficult to have with people! It's also a way for you to enjoy quality time with each other, which can be hard to come by if your anxious feelings or overthinking make the time you spend with each other difficult to enjoy.

Having covered these challenges, we're now ready to start looking more specifically at how you can overcome these triggers. The strategies we will be discussing in the next chapter will help you go from an overthinker to someone who is equipped with the tools to understand why you may think this way, what triggers you, and most importantly, what to do about it!

Chapter Five

Overcoming Overthinking Triggers

As we have seen in depth throughout the past few chapters, there are many reasons why you may be triggered by certain actions or behaviors (or lack thereof!) in your relationship. Anxiety and overthinking are tricky things to deal with, but that doesn't mean that they cannot be overcome. For the next chapters, we will be focusing exclusively on dealing with this anxiety, as you should, by now, have gained a solid understanding of the reasons behind these triggers and what makes you an anxious person.

Identifying Your Triggers

The very first step in overcoming your triggers will be to identify them. This sounds simple, but it will take some time to get used to. Let's think about the common ones: a breakdown in communication, feeling like you aren't being supported, jealousy or other insecurities, past traumas, and stressors that are external to the relationship.

Communication

Let's start by looking at communication. Communication, as we all know, is a pillar in relationships and is something that is necessary for everyone, not just the overthinker, to feel safe and secure. Communication is how you verbalize what you are thinking, how you discuss your feelings with your partner, how you navigate through conflict successfully and efficiently, and how you make sure that you are on the same page. It is also how you get to know each other! If you look back on the moment when you and your partner met, think about how much you used your communication to get to know each other. Think about how much you spoke about the things they like and dislike, what they do for a living, and so on. Then, think about the more subtle parts too, you may have paid attention to how they treat waiters at the restaurant. Then, you may have had your first disagreement or fight, and noticed how they act in these situations. Perhaps their communication helped you feel more secure, or maybe they made you feel like you weren't being listened to properly when you discussed your thoughts and feelings.

Communication happens all the time, even when we don't think it is. In fact, when we don't communicate, this is a form of communication in itself: we communicate that we are holding back from sharing some thoughts and ideas, albeit in an unproductive way that can only lead to more confusion. We may also be passive aggressive, not really saying how we feel directly, but saying it in a snarky way, which only confuses the other or which puts oil on the fire. There are many kinds of communication styles, and not all of them are the "proper" way to do so if we want to come to a common ground with someone. This is where many communication breakdowns happen, and where misunderstandings, or a lack of communication altogether, can lead to more problems than solutions. Indeed, a lack of communication can escalate into a much more significant trigger, and it can make you or your partner feel neglected, or even disrespected.

What is "good" communication, then? Good communication is honest and open. It involves you sharing how you feel in an honest manner, not holding back from openly sharing your emotions and feelings, and doing so in a way that is not passive aggressive. For instance, if you are in a relationship and your partner makes you feel like you aren't being heard, or like you aren't being taken care of, instead of saying "Well it's not like I matter to you anyways!", you would say "I feel like I need more care from you, I haven't been feeling great lately and I'd like to talk about how we can change that together." This form of communication is honest and open: you are sharing how you are feeling openly, and you are being honest and vulnerable.

You aren't judging the person or telling them that they are wrong; instead, you are focusing on how you feel, and how you would like to approach that subject. It's true that sometimes, the truth might be difficult to say and to hear, but it is still better to be honest with one another than to ignore how you are truly feeling. Ignoring the truth only delays the conversation, and by the time that you are honest with your partner, your emotions may be far higher, which makes it difficult to stay cool and collected when the conversation pops up.

Good communication also involves active listening. This is a form of listening in which you don't only listen to respond, but to really hear what the other person is saying. In anxious attachment styles, it is common for people to feel like any form of conflict represents a threat. The anxious person will tend to feel like any form of conflict means that the relationship as a whole is in the balance, while the securely attached person may feel like this is just a conversation like any other, but one that requires finding a common ground. This is why active listening can feel so difficult to do, the anxious person feels like they have to defend themselves, or they may feel like it's better to avoid the conflict altogether to keep the peace.

In non-confrontational situations, this may also be the case: the anxious person might prefer agreeing to what the other person is saying, or may avoid bringing up events that took place that made them feel poorly about themselves, because keeping the peace feels safer than bringing up a problem. Active listening is needed here, instead of listening to respond, listen to what your partner is saying without assuming things. I cannot stress this enough: if you aren't sure of what they say, mean, or imply with what they are saying, ask a question. Do not make comments or respond based on an assumption, as this can lead the partner to feel like they aren't being listened to. You can do this by paraphrasing, or repeating what they have said in your words to make sure that you have understood them correctly. This also includes acknowledging your partner's feelings and their perspectives, instead of shooting them down because they view things differently from the way that you view them.

Now, especially in moments where emotions are running high, active listening can be difficult because you or your partner may get lost in the conversation and may not fully understand what you are arguing about anymore if you have both been too focused on being right or on responding, instead of listening. In those moments, acknowledge that this is the case and try to be mindful. What are you talking about? What are you discussing? What is the key issue at hand that you are trying to solve together? How can you go about solving this in a way that makes you both feel good about yourselves and what you are trying to solve?

Next, pay attention to your nonverbal communication. We all communicate nonverbally with our body language, eye contact, touch, and so on. For example, rolling your eyes at something that your partner says is not inviting. It sends the message that you are not respectful of their perspective, and that you aren't listening to them with an open mind. Similarly, if you cross your legs and arms while listening to the person sharing their experience or thoughts with you, your body is showing closeness, which doesn't make the person feel like you are open to discussing these issues. You can recognize these cues too by looking at your partner's reactions.

Nonverbal communication also shows itself through touch. Now, you may not want a hug if you are in a conflict because your partner did something that crossed your boundaries, but if you are going through an argument because of miscommunication, you or your partner may want to touch each other, or hold each other's hands to show that you care about how they feel when going through this conflict.

This brings us to another component of good communication, which is showing empathy. Again, it can be difficult to be empathetic towards someone if you feel like they have wronged you, or like they do not really care about you or how you feel. However, a respectful partner will show empathy for how you are feeling. A caring partner will remain empathetic and kind towards you when you discuss things that you are unhappy with, or things that may hurt you. The same can be expected from you. Try to truly hear your partner's viewpoint, even if it differs a lot from your own, and try to express empathy for their feelings. You do not have to agree with them, but you can still show that you care about how they feel. This is a two-way street: show empathy and you will receive it too.

Your relationship will also have disagreement at times. After all, we are all different people with different viewpoints, perspectives, and ideas around how the world works. So, although you may hope, as an anxious person, that you will never disagree with your partner and vice versa, the chances of this happening are very low. That doesn't mean that your disagreements will always turn into fights, into heated arguments, or will lead to disrespect. Instead, having good communication with your partner requires you to engage in respectful disagreements.

This means approaching disagreements with respect by avoiding blame, critiquing the person personally, or holding them in contempt. Of course, you may disagree with things that are personal to you, treating you poorly, calling you names etc (although you shouldn't be with that person in the first place, but that's something to discuss in therapy) in which case although you want to come forward respectfully, you also do not want to allow yourself to be spoken to in a disrespectful way. As always, communication is a two-way street! If you struggle with this, try focusing on the issue that you are confronting, instead of the person. Comment on the behavior, not the person. Comment on the actions, not the person taking them.

Communication won't always be quick, and it will sometimes require you to be patient. Not all conversations can happen just anytime, part of communicating well with someone involves knowing when is the right time to talk about certain topics, and when it isn't.

For example, if your partner comes home after just having been laid off, that might not be the right time to bring up the fact that you feel like they haven't been very present with you lately. Instead, it's time to be empathetic and to be supportive, putting the other conversation on hold for a different time. The same can be expected from them with you. Then, during conversations themselves, both partners need to be patient and avoid jumping on another, or interrupting one another, because they feel like they cannot wait for the other to be done speaking before they share their perspective.

Then, communication should also include feedback and appreciation. You are there for each other, and you care about each other's feelings, make sure that you communicate this! You want each other to feel good about how the conversation ended, so take some time to show this to each other. This goes beyond just conflict situations, tell each other often that you appreciate each other, that you are grateful for what they do for you, and vice versa.

This communication will take a lot of effort, and it will take time for you two to find a way to speak to each other in ways that you can best understand each other. Your partnership is a place for you both to grow as partners, so don't throw in the towel if you feel like you struggle to communicate effectively right from the get-go. Give yourself and your partner! Grace. Make yourself and your wishes clear. If you are anxious because they don't communicate enough for your liking, explain this to them, being clear on what you would appreciate and why you would appreciate, but don't blame them for not knowing this.

A Perceived Lack of Effort

Another common trigger for anxiety might be that you feel like your partner isn't putting in enough effort into your relationship. You might feel like you are emotionally disconnected from each other, or you may even feel lonely at times. You might be physically together and still feel disconnected. Your partner might seem indifferent or unresponsive to your emotional needs, or might not give the right amount of care when something big happens in your life, a promotion, your birthday, and so on. This is where your communication comes in, you need to communicate these things in a kind way. You can also ask your partner whether this is something that they do with intent, or whether they don't know how much effort you would like them to put in. Again, try not to come at this from a perspective of "they're doing this intentionally" which can lead you to start a conversation that blames them. Try to understand instead, and make your needs clear to them. What do you need them to do differently to feel better?

You could also be feeling this way if the conversations you are having feel mainly one-sided, and like they are showing little interest or engagement for you or what you are doing. For example, your partner might interrupt you, dismiss your concerns, or might try to shift the focus away from you when you discuss concerns, instead focusing it on them. These are real issues to address, again by speaking in "I statements" and focusing on how it is making you feel. Sharing these issues is one thing, how your partner reacts can either help you or make you feel like you aren't being validated, which is a different problem to address.

Your partner may also offer very minimal practical assistance. They may leave a lot of the housework to you, or they might not seem to care when you seem to be overwhelmed. They might not be involved when you are planning things, dates, events, etc., or when you need to make important decisions, which can make you feel anxious as you start to wonder why they do not care. Similarly, if your partner isn't showing you much encouragement, you may feel like you aren't a partnership, but rather two people who happen to be together. Your partner might not encourage you in your goals, might not celebrate your accomplishments, or might dismiss you when you overcome challenges, all reasons why you might feel dismissed and like your partner isn't showing you the kind of care and support you would like to receive. These are normal reasons to feel anxious or to overthink.

Jealousy and Insecurities

We all get jealous from time to time. Yes, even you, the people who say they "don't get jealous." We get jealous if we feel like something is threatening our relationship, or threatening to change its dynamics. We may also feel jealous of our partners if we feel like they are less attached to us than we are to them, we may feel jealous that they aren't as dependent on us as we are on them.

Jealousy, and especially insecurities tends to stem from past experiences with traumas, past insecurities, comparing ourselves to others, or from a lack of trust. For example, you may be jealous if your partner goes away on vacation and is surrounded by people that you fear they may cheat on you with. This may be because you have experienced something like this before, or because you have insecurities that make you feel like you may not be good enough for your partner. Indeed, feeling inadequate, having low self-esteem, having personal issues that you haven't resolved yet, or generally feeling like your partner is settling for you may make you anxious because you fear that they may "find someone better."

Trauma is a big player here too. If you've dealt with partners who were unfaithful, or partners who reinforced your insecurities by treating you poorly, even the best partner could make you feel insecure. Your partner may be caring, may be giving you attention, may call you while on vacation to keep the example from above, and you may still feel anxious that they aren't being truthful or that they are only going to be interested in you for a limited period of time. The result? You might try to "tighten the rope" around your partner, constantly wanting more communication or more reassurance, or constantly trying to prove to them that you are worthy of their love, even if this anxiety stems from you and is unfounded when we look at the dynamics in your relationship. If trauma is the reason behind your insecurities and jealousy, it is something to uncover in therapy.

In this day and age, we also have access to social media, which is a breeding ground for comparison. We are constantly shown other people doing amazing things, which can make it hard to rationalize the fact that we are only seeing a version of their life, and not the whole picture. Likewise, it creates a bias: we only see the people who choose to show their lives, not the others who, like you, might live a life that is drastically different from what you are seeing online. Whether you compare yourself to others online, picking at your differences and wishing you looked different or led a different life, or whether you look at other couples and feel like your partner doesn't act the way that others do, it doesn't matter, all forms of comparison poison the mind to an extent, because it puts an idea of what's "right" or the "goal" while dismissing the fact that 99% of what we see online is unrealistic.

Finally, you may simply have a lack of trust, whether that stems from your personal history or your current relationship dynamics. Every relationship is different, so you might be with someone who is very trustworthy, or may be with someone who has breached your trust once and therefore have a harder time trusting them now. A lack of trust in your partner can make it very difficult to find ways around dealing with the anxiety you feel, so this is something to discuss with them and potentially in therapy if you find that you cannot address these issues effectively between you and your partner alone.

Stressors External to Your Relationship

Last but not least, stress can be a ginormous source of anxiety, but especially if it comes from outside your relationship. After all, many divorces in the United States are caused by financial stress, as well as a lack of family support or dealing with too much conflict. These are all stressful situations, which create the perfect storm in which a relationship may end. Emotional spillovers, for example, can cause you to feel anxious around your relationship. If you are very emotional because things aren't doing great at work, you may bring these emotions into your relationship. Similarly, if your partner is generally unhappy with their current life, this unhappiness may manifest as extra stress brought into the relationship, even if you are the happiest part of their life. The minute someone brings negative external emotions into the relationship, your interactions and moods are likely to change with them. For a person with an anxious attachment style, it can be extremely stressful to see this and even more difficult not to attribute these mood changes to you or your relationship going through a challenging time, which again, can be a trigger for anxiety.

More stress can also come with less quality time. A new job, changing jobs, getting bad news about a family member, these are all external stressors that may have a significant impact on you, your partner, or both of you. High levels of external stress can make it hard to have quality time together, which may make you feel like you are disconnected from your partner. You might want to enjoy some down time together, might want to spend time doing fun things, but if you are not in an emotional or mental state to do so, you may feel like your relationship starts to be affected by this. In those moments, try to separate the event from the emotion. There are stressors, acknowledge them. Focus on keeping the relationship supportive, and try to disconnect the relationship from the stressor. These stressors, more often than not, will pass, and your relationship will survive, even if your partner isn't as upbeat as usual. Keep this in mind too if you feel like the stress is starting to affect your communication style. Short tempers, withdrawals, a lack of communication, these are all the kinds of changes to communication you might notice if emotions are running high. Speak to your partner about this and be mindful together of the impact that these stressors could be having on your conversations and general communication.

Finally, physical and mental health strains can strain your relationship because of exhaustion or increased anxiety and depression. This is something that you, as a couple, can work on together, by acknowledging the moment and understanding that you may need to support each other more than usual.

Before you continue reading, take a moment to consider these triggers and try to identify which ones you felt closely related to your situation. Is a lack of communication something that triggers anxiety and overthinking? Is it a change in patterns? Is it stress? Is your partner's lack of effort affecting your anxiety, making you question whether they are invested in this relationship? You don't need to have a specific list just yet, as this is what we will work on in the next section. For now, try to have a quick think about the ones you relate to the most.

Uncovering Your Triggers and Stressors

We have discussed the main trigger points, so now, it's time for a few exercises to help you understand yourself better.

Reflective Journaling

The first is reflective journaling, which is where you start thinking about the events in which you have strong emotional reactions. We are full of thoughts (as you will know, as an overthinker), but we also tend to just jump past these thoughts without taking the time to think about what they mean, or the greater implications they may have on our lives. Journaling offers you a way to reflect on your thoughts so you can go beyond just facing or admitting your feelings, and so you can properly process them. Writing down your thoughts gives you a methodical way to dissect them so you can understand what they are caused by, and the effects they have.

You get to process what is happening around you and then break them down. Think about it, when we "work something out," "figure something out," or "sort something out," we are processing things. We are breaking things down in a way that we better understand them. When we journal, we deconstruct and examine situations in our lives, or even emotions themselves, to uncover what parts of these emotions and situations are having an effect on us. We internalize these problems and get to break them down into more digestible pieces so we can equally address these.

The great part in this is that we get to get rid of built-up feelings that would otherwise stay deep within us, at least until we can't keep them in anymore. So, journaling gives us that opportunity to think about the situations, problems, and emotions that are more deeply ingrained into us so we can start understanding them on a deeper level. So, it is a self-reflection tool that you can use to identify the situations that trigger your anxiety. And hey, don't just take my word for it! Research has shown that journaling is a "low-cost, low-side effect therapy that can help family physicians in the management of common mental health symptoms." Research has additionally shown that keeping record of our thoughts and feelings especially helps us by reducing anxiety, helping us take a step back from obsessive thinking or ruminating, and can help improve our awareness of events so we have better clarity and understanding of what is happening and what to do next.

To journal, you don't need many materials. You just need a pen and a piece of paper, or you can do it digitally, and then need to start writing. There are a few ways in which you can do this. For example, you can start by picking a situation in which you felt especially triggered. Think about that moment, and try to think about what the context was. Be as precise as you can be. Where were you, and what were you doing before you started to feel anxious? What happened next, and what was the first emotion you felt? What did you do when you first started feeling this way? Then, did the anxiety start feeling better, or did it keep getting worse? What kind of coping skills did you use? What do you think made you feel worse or better?

Another option you have is to write in a "stream of consciousness." The stream of consciousness is a psychological concept introduced by William James in the 1800s. In the context of writing, it is a process in which we write without holding ourselves back, and with full freedom.

114

It is written in a non-linear way, so we write things down as they come to our minds, and we don't think about what happens next. Sometimes, with journaling, we can get stuck thinking about what to write, but the stream of consciousness helps you get past this because it is a style of writing in which you do not care about the organization, the narrative, the punctuation or grammar, and whether it makes sense, you just write. You can set up a timer if this helps you, start with ten minutes. Then, once the ten minutes are over, have a look at what you have written, and try to find some patterns or interesting thoughts. These can show you thoughts that you may not have thought you had.

Try to journal in a way that helps you identify what made you triggered or what made you feel this way. Try to be as descriptive as possible. Then, pick up on the cues, and pay attention to them next time you start feeling like a trigger might be happening.

Feedback Loops

The next option you have is called a feedback loop, and it is exactly what it sounds like: you talk to your partner about the trigger and you try to figure out what happened. This should be an open discussion with your partner about a moment of tension, or a moment in which you felt very anxious, and then listen to their perspective so you can better understand how they viewed the situation. Then, you can discuss together how to avoid these the next time this happens. You can also take this opportunity to ask your partner how they would like you to communicate this with them so they do not feel like you are pushing your anxiety onto them. Do they want you to share it with them when you are anxious? Do they prefer that you speak to someone else first and wait until you have calmed down? How do you feel about that?

Therapy

Again, therapy can come in greatly handy here! A therapist can help you understand your emotional responses better, as well as their origins. They can help you understand why some things trigger you while others do not, and they can explore potential solutions with you. Therapy can also be a place for you to share your thoughts with someone who does not judge you, and therefore, a place where you can practice setting boundaries, sharing your perspective of events, and practice how you will bring up a conversation with your partner if you are anxious about starting difficult conversations.

As a couple, therapy can also help you navigate these tough conversations if you have tried to uncover your triggers but to no avail. This is a place where you can feel safe in exploring these emotions and where, again, a middleman is there to help keep the peace if things get heated.

Mindfulness Practices

Anxiety is a feeling in which we can get lost. We can easily feel overwhelmed by our thoughts because they are powerful. Anxiety can blind us and make us read into things when nothing is really happening. We may be aware that we are just being anxious, and that we need to rationalize things. But being rational when anxious is very hard, which is where mindfulness comes in. Mindfulness, as a practice, invites you to be more aware of your emotional state so you can recognize the onset of a response to a trigger before this response escalates. Essentially, this means being mindful of how you feel, and knowing when you start to have that ping of anxiety in your stomach.

For example, you can try an exercise in which you breathe mindfully and perform what we call a "sensory engagement." Start by centering your breath. For this, close your eyes, and take in slow, deep breaths. Inhale through your nose, and let your chest expand fully. Then, exhale through your mouth. Only focus on the breath that is coming into your lungs, and focus on how it feels as it leaves your body. Then, start doing a "body scan," which is where you start from the top of your head and move down to your toes. As you move down your body, mentally scan yourself and find areas of tension. Then, imagine breathing into them and letting the tension melt away with every breath you take. Next, engage your senses. Still keeping your eyes closed, look for colors, patterns, or light that appears from behind your eyelids. Next, focus on what you can hear. What noises are in your immediate surroundings? Do you hear buzzing around you? Then, focus on the smell. Are there odors or scents in the air that you can pick up on? Let them come and go. Next, taste. Pay attention to the taste in your mouth, or how your tongue feels. And finally, touch. What is the temperature like? Can you feel the air moving on your skin? Before finishing the exercise, take a few moments to take in the silence, listening to your breath.

Managing and Minimizing Triggers

I have had many clients over the years who have come to me seeking help for their anxious thoughts, and while I cannot tell you specific stories, I can give you some ideas of the kinds of experiences they went through with their partners. For example, there have been many times where clients have been so overwhelmed by triggers that they felt they were completely at a loss of control with their mind and body. Their partner's communication had changed drastically and they couldn't calm themselves down.

Emotional Regulation Skills

Let's imagine a scenario together. Think about a woman called Annette. Annette's partner, on a sabbatical year, decided to leave for around five weeks to go travel on his own in a country far away where the time difference was over five hours. Over the first one or two weeks of her partner being gone, Annette was doing great, she had time to do things that she hadn't previously had time for because of the time commitment her partner represented, and she had a fantastic time doing all kinds of things with all that extra time. During those first few weeks, the communication was great. All was going well, until one night, when her partner seemed to be distant, not responsive to her messages, or took ages to answer. Immediately, her mind went to the worst case scenarios, he was cheating, or he was out with other girls that he would find better than her, or he was outright ignoring her because she was annoying, the list went on.

The more Annette thought of these scenarios, the more anxious she became. She had a hard time focusing at work, instead spending time looking meticulously through his list of followers on Instagram to stalk any new followers.

The scenarios kept going in her mind, thinking of all the things he could be doing. She did the math: his last message was at 6 PM local time, and now it was 12PM the next day. He still hadn't said good morning even though he had been online, so that was it. The relationship was over. He had found someone better. She started getting angry, sad, overwhelmed by these thoughts, and the more she thought, the more she found herself confused with what was reality versus what she was imagining. She had been talking to a friend for support, telling her that he was being weird or distant, so much so that she started to believe her own anxious thoughts, which had previously only been question marks in her head. She didn't want to call him out on it and be the "clingy girlfriend" but she also knew that it couldn't continue like this.

Then, her partner texted, though only vaguely, adding to this anxiety. Then, she started re-reading the messages they had been exchanging with one another, looking through the last few days to spot any inconsistencies, only to find that he had been pretty consistent. He had said good morning and good night every day. He had called her almost every day. He had sent pictures of his trip. He had asked her how she was feeling, what she was up to, and for general news. Slowly, Annette felt even more upset, how much of her anxiety had been self-inflicted, based on assumptions, or smaller pings of anxiety that had snowballed into a full-blown trigger? Exhausted from all these feelings and overwhelmed, she decided to sleep on it.

The next day, Annette realized that most of this anxiety had indeed started as a small thing: lack of communication. What felt incredibly overwhelming and overpowering was primarily the power of her thoughts, which had made a small trigger, no goodnight text, into a huge, unmanageable ball of emotion. She told her partner that she would appreciate keeping the routine in the future, not mentioning anxiety, and suddenly, this never happened again.

But how can such small triggers lead to such humongous reactions? Well, for many people like Annette, this results from bad experiences in the past that have made them extremely anxious at the sight of a potential problem. For others, it may be past trauma. The triggers you have may be different from Annette, but they can have the exact same impact, and that's exhausting for you to deal with.

What Annette needed in that moment was better emotional regulation skills, which are skills that help us relax and take back control of our emotions. For example, these may include deep breathing, as we did in the previous exercise. They can also include meditation, where you focus on the feelings you feel, the sensations in your body, and try to enter into a meditative state. You could also try progressive muscle relaxation so you can manage your physiological responses. The goal is to find a way to relax your body and your mind, and to focus on what's real, versus what is coming from a place of anxiety. Annette found some relief in looking for evidence for the sources of her stress, she looked for signs that would contradict her feelings.

This is something you can do too by asking yourself what evidence you have for the anxious feelings you have and what evidence you have that contradicts this. Annette, for example, found that reminding herself that her partner made an effort every day before this was comforting. She also found comfort in making her needs clear afterwards, she wanted to have a good morning and a good night next to have a better idea of her partner's schedule, what he was up to, and so on. However, emotional regulation skills can be hard to develop without help, so don't hesitate to look for professional help so you can combat this.

Enhancing Your Communication

Many anxiety triggers come as a result of poor communication, as we saw earlier. Therefore, a direct solution to this is to have a way to communicate with your partner that helps you reduce your anxiety. Structured dialogue is one such way. This is a process by which you implement a structured communication format to adhere to when you discuss sensitive topics, making sure that both you and your partner feel heard and understood. As discussed, moments of high stress can feel extremely overwhelming, which can lead to poorer communication. Having this kind of communication format can give you the guidance you may need to have a conversation that doesn't feel too stressful and therefore, that leads to a more productive outcome. This structure can include, for example, putting time aside to discuss without interruptions, using "I" statements, being actively mindful of your active listening, and so on. You can also follow conflict resolution training if you feel that your conflicts have been unproductive.

Part of enhancing your communication also involves working on the foundations of your relationship. As we've seen, trust is a crucial part of your relationship. You may need to do some trust-building activities where you communicate your triggers and concerns with your partner, and where they can respond and support you. These activities do not have to be solely focused on triggers, building trust in general with help with this too. For example, you can add a few more activities to do together to your schedule, go on a vacation together, and so on.

Check-ins have also been shown to work well in people who are anxious. You can discuss this with your partner to see what kind of check-ins you would like, and what you would like to discuss. This can be a check in about the health of your relationship, what you think works well and what doesn't work as well. You could also discuss upcoming stressful moments that you will need to support each other through, and the needs or concerns you feel need to be touched on. These check-ins can help you by preventing potential triggers and giving you a greater feeling of safety so you know exactly what to expect.

On a final note, anxiety can feel extremely overwhelming at times, but by identifying your triggers, you can start to overcome them. Focus on identifying them so you can prevent them from taking place, and you'll be one step ahead the whole way. That being said, there are other tools we can use to address this, including thought reframing, which we will discuss in the next chapter.

Chapter Six

Reframing Negative Thought Patterns

Overthinking happens because we have thoughts that trigger more and more of these thoughts in a disruptive way. We think one thing, which makes us think about it more, and more, and more, until we get lost in these thoughts and overwhelmed by the emotions that come with them. A solution for this, then, is to reframe these thoughts to stop the overthinking pattern altogether. This is what we will be exploring throughout this chapter. But first, let's think about what negative thought patterns are. These kinds of thoughts are the ones that make you feel worse about yourself or the situation you are in, even if they are not accurate or realistic.

Identifying and Challenging Cognitive Distortions

There are different kinds of negative thought patterns. For example, overgeneralizing when a situation is only happening in that very moment is a common pattern. We might have a situation where, like Annette, our partner does something that we dislike, a change in communication patterns, and we think to ourselves "this always happens!" So, we feel like that negative thing happens all the time, when in reality, this is a rare thing that has only happened once or twice. Overgeneralizing then makes us more anxious, because we start thinking about other moments that looked similar, even if they weren't. Another such form is living by rules of "shoulds" and "musts," which are rules that you set for yourself that you also hold yourself accountable to.

These kinds of rules create a frame around which you base how you think you should act, or should have acted. Then, by creating these kinds of rules, you also set yourself up for failure because you hold yourself up to standards that you feel you cannot miss. You judge yourself for not fulfilling your own rules. These shoulds and musts can also be applied to other people, which can make it exhausting for others to abide by. They may feel like they have rules to fulfill, or else, they are letting you down. This is similar to labeling, which is when you pass a judgment on yourself without proof. For example, after a breakup, you might say to yourself, "I'm just not good enough" when in reality, this is not about you personally, but about the relationship itself not working out.

When Thoughts Are Inaccurate

Other similar thought patterns include discounting the positive, jumping to conclusions, and splitting (or black-and-white thinking). Unfortunately, as human beings, we naturally have a tendency to focus on the negative, this is called the negativity bias. Essentially, this means that we tend to see the negative and to focus more on that than on positives. So, add distortions to this and we have positivity discounting. Although great things are happening, we discount the positive to focus instead on the negative. So, we focus on that negativity, unaware that focusing on it makes it feel a lot more real, and a lot more difficult to overcome.

Then, we may also jump to conclusions, assuming things which are usually the worst-case scenario, without thinking about the other potential outcomes, and without knowing all the facts. So, like Annette, we may assume that our partner is being unfaithful or is losing interest, when in reality, they might just be busy (yes, really). Finally, there's black-or-white thinking, where we forget to see the gray area, which includes all the other possibilities. We only see extremes, you are wrong, or correct. You are good or bad. They are happy in the relationship, or their mood seems less chirpy than usual, so the relationship is ending soon.

Make Them More Accurate

These contortions affect how we view the world and consequently our relationships. If we don't work hard to change them, they can also lead to our relationships breaking down altogether, as it can affect the decisions we make. So, it starts with awareness. For this, return to chapter five and try out the journaling exercise, this time focusing on your contortions. Can you see in these entries whether you may have used such a distortion? Were you perhaps too pessimistic about something that could have been viewed in a different way, with more nuance? You can also use meditation to become more aware of these thoughts, or mindfulness, as we saw earlier.

A different option is to question the evidence. When you have these thoughts, instead of assuming that they are relevant and true, ask yourself the kind of evidence you have that supports these thoughts. Are they legitimate, or do they stem solely from an emotion that has been triggered by an event that usually triggers you? What evidence do you have for them? What evidence might counter-argue this?

You can also apply the double-standard method, which is when you ask yourself, "Would I say this to a friend?" This gets you to think about the way you are speaking to yourself and about yourself. Most people want to avoid hurting other people, so we try to avoid telling them things that we know could hurt their feelings. And yet, although we are the only friend we are guaranteed to ever have for the rest of our life, we are also our harshest critics. Think about whether the thoughts you are having are some you would want a friend to have. Would you feel sad to see them speaking about themselves in this way? Would you prefer that they give themselves a bit more credit, that they cut themselves some slack? If this is what you expect for your friends, shouldn't you expect the same for yourself? This method helps you highlight the harsh criticism you might be using, and it helps you have a kinder and more balanced perspective.

And finally, you can try the perspective shift method, where you put yourself in the shoes of an outsider when thinking about yourself and your situations. This can help you gain a more objective view of your thoughts and behaviors, and can help you put a finger down on the cause of your overthinking.

Reframing Your Thoughts

Beyond these methods, there are other specific ways in which you can reframe the thoughts you have so they are more positive, optimistic, and encouraging. One of these methods is the power of using the word "yet." In this method, you are encouraged to add the word "yet" to what you are saying, so that instead of saying a definitive statement that closes the opportunity for any further improvement, you acknowledge that the thought you are having is temporary. For example, you may say, "I can't do this yet" instead of saying that you cannot do this at all, and therefore, that there is no option to change this. This won't work on every sentence, but it can help with some.

Exposure Therapy

You can also gradually expose yourself to fears or situations in which your thoughts tend to be negative. This requires you to be aware of the situations that trigger you so you can carefully put yourself in these situations while being prepared to confront them. Again, this isn't a method that will fit all situations, and it should only be done in situations where you are in enough control of the situation that you can gradually expose yourself without undergoing a full trigger that you cannot come back from easily. This can especially help you confront situations where you catastrophize things, as through practice, you get to see how the situations that you normally would catastrophize turn out much less catastrophic than you initially anticipated.

Is There Another Explanation?

You could also try using alternative explanations. This is especially useful for distortions around personalization and jumping to conclusions. Personalization refers to when we speak negatively about ourselves and blame ourselves for situations we have very little control over. Instead of blaming yourself or jumping to the conclusion that you are to blame, try to find alternative reasons why something may be happening. Could it be because of the circumstances? Could it be something that is outside your control? List different reasons why this very thing could be happening, and focus on these, instead of on yourself.

What Are the Best and Worst-Case Scenarios?

Another option is the best-worst-realistic outcome analysis in which you analyze a situation by considering what the best, worst, and most realistic outcomes are. This can help you rationalize a situation when you are catastrophizing it. For example, let's imagine that you are Annette, and that you are thinking of all the potential worst-case scenarios that could explain your partner's changed communication. What would be the best case scenario? What would be the worst case scenario? What is most likely to be the most realistic, based on what you know about them and the kind of person they are?

Self-Talk and Self-Compassion

We truly are our harshest critics. The number of times that I have had clients who speak to themselves in incredibly harsh ways is too large to count. And yet, as mentioned earlier, we are our only guaranteed best friend for the rest of our lives. Whatever happens next, we will always be by our own sides. So, doesn't it make sense to make sure that the relationship we have with ourselves is the strongest of all? Unfortunately, overthinking often comes in the way of this, making it far easier or more natural to think about ourselves in a negative light than to be kind to ourselves. We are quick to find things about ourselves, and yet, finding something about ourselves that we like and even cherish seems to be a difficult task. As we have seen throughout this book, insecurities, low self-esteem, and low confidence all lead to a propensity to overthink because instead of being self-assured and trusting ourselves in how we think or feel, we speak poorly of ourselves. We think poorly of ourselves. We view ourselves in the most negative of lights, not giving us any grace or the benefit of the doubt. For overthinking patterns to change, we need to change your thoughts, and that starts with the thoughts you have about yourself.

Be Kinder to Yourself

Let's begin by identifying some of your positive attributes. Think about all the things that you like about yourself. If none come to mind, think about what other people have said about you, and what you agree with. Now, take some more time and dig deep, what do you like about your personality and about how you treat people? What do you like about the way you act with others? What do you like about what you do in life, such as your career, your accomplishments, and so on? It might feel weird to think about these because it is different from what you usually do, but give yourself the space to do this. It's important to rewire the way you speak about yourself and to focus on positive things instead of just looking at the negatives. You should build a solid foundation for positive self-talk, and that starts with knowing what you love about yourself.

Next, we will do a self-compassion exercise, which again, might feel weird, especially if you tend to blame yourself a lot for various reasons. Specifically, the task is to write a letter to yourself from a compassionate friend's perspective, where you look at yourself from the outside and tell yourself all kinds of great things. Think about the way you would write a letter to your best friend, and do this for yourself. What kind of compliments would you give yourself? What accomplishments would you congratulate yourself for? What were the best moments you spent together? Write this letter only focusing on the positives, leaving aside the things that you may not be as happy with.

Change Your Perspective

Your next exercise is to write down a few personal mantras and positive affirmations. An affirmation is something that you want for yourself, such as something you want to do, the kind of person you want to be, where you want to see yourself in the future, and so on. These affirmations can be short and sweet, as long as they mean something to you. For example, think of an affirmation about your confidence. This could be "I am a confident person today, period." Make sure to add the "today" and "period" because it signals to your brain that this information is about who you are now, not about who you will become. You can also focus on things you want to improve and make an affirmation out of them. For example, if you have past traumas relating to relationships you were in previously that turned out to be destructive, such as relationships in which you felt disrespected, an affirmation could be "I am worthy of respect today, period." These affirmations are there for you to remind yourself of the kind of treatment you deserve, how you want people to treat you, and therefore, boost your self-esteem.

Remember the negativity bias? Now's the time to address it. Your brain, as mentioned earlier, has a negativity bias in which it focuses on negative experiences instead of positive ones. Now that you know this, make the conscious effort to focus on positive experiences and emotions instead. This can be done through gratitude journaling, where you take a few minutes each day to write down a few things you are grateful for. You can also overcome this bias by being mindful of the moments where you feel especially happy, take a moment to really take it in, and note how you feel. What makes you feel this good, and how can you bring more of it into your life?

Finally, look at the community you have around you and ask yourself whether these are the kinds of people that you want in your life, whether they make you feel good, and whether you feel like they are your cheerleaders. We all deserve to be respected, but oftentimes, people who have low self-esteem or who do not believe that they are worthy of being respected may end up surrounding themselves with people who treat them as such. So, look at who you are surrounded with. Do they push you up? Do they support you? Do they talk about you in a positive manner, or do you often feel less-than when you are around them? Your friends and support system are a mirror for your own worth and abilities, so choose them wisely.

It will be a tricky transition at first, but the more you practice changing these cognitive distortions, the more it will become a habit. Take it day by day, practice the exercises and techniques provided above, and you will start to see gradual changes.

Chapter Seven

Establishing Healthy Boundaries

Over the years, you have most likely heard a lot about boundaries. This is a concept that has grown especially quickly in popularity over the past few years due to the spread of social media. What used to be something that we could only access by speaking to professionals, namely quick access to insights in psychology, has now become something that we can access incredibly easily. There are pros and cons to this, on the one hand, seeing these posts might have helped you gain a better understanding of what boundaries are, how they can help you have a healthier relationship, or even be a better partner.

On the other hand, this kind of content can make us therapize our conversations, making the conversations we have with people feel disconnected from what we actually mean, as we are, instead, focusing primarily on saying words that might mean great things, but that do not actually connect well with our partner. We end up speaking to our partner as though they are a patient, instead of our partner, and that just makes the communication very cold between the two of us.

What Are Boundaries?

Boundaries are essential in your relationships, whether with a partner or with your friends. They are the guidelines that we use to explain to others how we wish to be treated by other people. They aren't just about defining what's appropriate or inappropriate (in your eyes) but they also tell you and the people you have relationships with what your values are, the needs you have, and your limits. These are incredibly important in any relationship, but especially in your romantic ones, because they are how you can have a healthy interaction dynamic with your partner. They are how you can feel safe and respected.

Your boundaries can be emotional, physical, mental, or even time-related! Emotional boundaries, for example, are all about protecting your feelings and making sure that you are respecting your limits by avoiding overextending yourself. For example, if you have a friend who constantly comes to you looking for help with their emotions but you aren't in a place where you can help them because you are going through something yourself, you would need to put a boundary and tell that person that you aren't capable of helping them right then and there.

Next, you have physical boundaries which are about your privacy, your personal space, and your body. You might not be a hugger, or you might not like being touched in certain places. You might not appreciate PDA, or might only be comfortable with hand-holding while in public. Setting boundaries here is important so you aren't in uncomfortable situations, whether it's to please your partner, or if it's because you think this is what you are expected to do. Remember: it's okay to have boundaries. They're there for a good reason, to keep you feeling safe.

Then, we also have mental or intellectual boundaries relating to what you accept in terms of values. You have more conservative values and want a partner that has those too? That's okay. You want someone more progressive? That's fine as well. You are allowed to have things that you believe in and things that you disagree with, and you are also allowed to choose to stick to people who respect those values. Indeed, your boundaries are there for your own self-awareness and self-respect. In your relationship, they will help you maintain your identity so you can fully be yourself without feeling the need to be someone else to be accepted. If you feel like your partner isn't respecting or accepting you for who you are, boundaries are there to help you realize that you are not the problem, but that you might just not be compatible.

Boundaries Shouldn't Be "Shoulds" and "Musts"

Boundaries is a concept that has been gaining a lot of traction, and for good reasons. Unfortunately, many people go through life completely without boundaries, simply focusing on ensuring that their partners, friends, family members, and everyone else around them except for themselves, are always happy. As you can imagine, it's a pretty exhausting situation to be in. On the one hand, you want to keep everyone around you happy at all times, but on the other hand, you aren't being catered for. You don't feel like people care as much about how you feel as you do for others. It might start feeling rather one-sided, like you aren't really getting the attention you need, all while giving 110% of your energy to everyone around you. And then, when it comes to you, you're left annoyed and disappointed that others aren't doing what they should be doing.

Perhaps you picked up on the last sentence, or more specifically, a word in that last sentence that we discussed in the previous section. Take a minute to guess what it is. Got it? That's right, the shoulds. Unfortunately, in relationships, boundaries can become mixed up with the shoulds and the musts that we set for ourselves and for others. It can become pretty exhausting pretty quickly. For example, you may set up a rule for yourself and apply it to others, and when they do not respect that rule, which is a rule that you have set for yourself or others, they disappoint you, and you feel disrespected. This is a cognitive dysfunction, but it is also something that many people with an anxious attachment style have. Why? Because it gives them a feeling of control. It makes them feel like they are in control of the situation, or like they can control what they do, how others act, and the like. It gives them, and perhaps you, the feeling that they have a list of rules to abide by to offset the chaos that they tend to have grown up in.

In other words, take a statement like the following: if I make sure to always be there for my friends because that's what friends do, then my friends should do this for me too. If they don't do so, they're not good friends. What's the problem with that statement? There are a few. First, the person is assuming that they must always be there for their friends, no matter what. Then, subconsciously or consciously, they apply that rule to others too, creating a 'should' statement that others have to abide by, otherwise, they are at risk of disappointing you. This is a big load to carry for friends and partners alike, because they may feel like they constantly need to be on their best behavior to

141

remain friends with you, or more specifically to avoid upsetting you.

Now, you may think that some of your 'shoulds' are just boundaries, but this isn't necessarily the case for every situation. Some 'shoulds' are good, your partner should communicate well with you, you should be respectful towards your friends by using polite language, etc. However, other 'shoulds' are not good and may come across as being controlling or even manipulative, such as the examples given above, expecting that others will act like you because you give yourself that rule. The rule you give yourself does not need to be the same for everyone. In fact, this rule is simply one that you have given yourself, and unless it is something that you feel strongly about, it does not mean that it has to be abided by other people.

Boundaries Are a Two-Way Street

I often see people talking about boundaries as though they are something that only come from one person and need to be respected by others. Of course, they are there for you to feel good about yourself and to feel respected by your partner, but this doesn't mean that they must be respected. Instead, your boundaries are there for you to spot which kind of behaviors you accept, and which ones you do not accept, showing you whether the person you are with is someone who aligns with those boundaries. If someone refuses to respect them, or if someone constantly feels the need to bypass your boundaries, it might be time to consider whether you are a good match. We all have different boundaries depending on the things that we care a lot about. Some of us will care more about punctuality, while others will care more about showing a lot of interest in others, while other people's boundaries will be around physical touch (we all have that one friend who is not a big hugger!). These boundaries, especially in relationships, help you set up your expectations and share these with your partners to ensure that you feel safe and cared for, and to ensure that your partner knows what's expected of them.

Therefore, boundaries are a two-way street. You can make your boundaries clear with your partner, but that does not mean that they must abide by them. If they don't, that's when you need to think about whether the relationship is working, or whether you aren't a match. In fact, they are there for you and your partner to avoid being emotionally burned out. Instead of feeling like you need to constantly do what's needed to keep your partner happy, or instead of feeling as though you are always responsible for keeping the peace, you can share your boundaries with one another so you know from the get-go what to avoid doing, and what they prefer.

As you can imagine, this is especially helpful in regards to overthinking. Wouldn't you prefer knowing how to act and what to avoid doing to ensure that your partner feels safe and respected, instead of having to take guesses? Indeed, it's more comforting to know that some behaviors are acceptable, and to be reassured that your partner knows what you need to feel good in your relationship, than to constantly be doing your best to keep them happy by following your 'shoulds' and assuming that they apply to them too. Speak to your partner about what they think their boundaries might be, and share this moment together. How can you make sure that you will do what you can to keep each other happy and feeling safe? Having these boundaries will help you feel like your needs and desires are being fulfilled, instead of ignored or even overridden.

But It's Hard to Set Them!

I cannot tell you the number of times that I have had people in my office tell me that as hard as they tried to set boundaries, they just couldn't do it. It's understandable, especially for a person with an anxious attachment style: setting boundaries might feel as though you are setting your relationship on fire because you feel like your partner is going to leave you if you show the slightest sign of being unhappy. With anxiety, and especially when you are overthinking, you may feel like if you set a boundary, you are effectively telling your partner that that's it, it doesn't work. Let me paint a clearer picture for you.

Meet Gina, a 27-year old woman who has a history of being in bad relationships. Gina grew up in a household that was rather toxic. Her mother, a narcissist (as Gina would find out later in her mid-twenties), had a habit of constantly telling Gina off for whatever she would do. Gina was good at basketball? Her mother would ridicule her when she came home in her jersey. Gina liked to sing? Her mother would avoid giving her compliments, telling her "well, I guess you sing better than the singers of that song, but that's about it" when Gina showed her all the hard work she had been putting in when perfecting her rendition of the classic High School Musical "Breaking Free." As a kid, Gina didn't think much of it, she just did things a certain way to try and make her mother proud of her. She would accept the half compliments because they were better than the flat-out insults she would get.

Gina's mom was also obsessed with her weight, and decided to transfer that onto her child from a young age. Sometimes putting Gina on the scale as early as when she turned six, she would tell her, You'd be so much prettier if you lost a bit of weight here and there. Gina didn't get it,

145

she ran with her friends all the time, she had friends, she sang, she played basketball, and she was a star student, so what else could she do to make her mother happy?

Gina spent most of her childhood figuring out ways to keep her mother happy. When making jokes wasn't acceptable, she would stay quiet. When being quiet didn't work, she tried to take as little space as possible. When that didn't work either, she would just accept that her mother was in a bad mood that day, and would take whatever her mom would throw at her, words and more. As a result, she became an expert at responding to her mother's cues, never knowing what mood she would be in that day. She would try to read the room, and try to avoid doing things that would trigger her, sometimes successfully, but rarely so. It was unpredictable and of course, chaotic.

So, as Gina grew up and started dating, she began to replicate what she had seen her entire life and the relationship types she had had as a model: chaotic and unpredictable. Whenever someone would love-bomb her, giving her a lot of attention and showering her with appreciation, even if she knew that it was too soon and that the person was acting as though they had been dating for months, she loved in. It brought her back to her younger self, when her mother was in a great mood. That's when things were going so well, her mother was happy, and so was the rest of the family. And then, the cycle would repeat itself, she would be unhappy, mean, and cruel. But Gina knew that one day, the happy mother she knew would be back and would be nice to her, as long as she played nice and avoided triggering her.

So, Gina did the same in those relationships. Setting a boundary was considered close to impossible, because if she had dared telling her mother to stop doing something, she would stomp heavily, run away, scream, or else. Gina had learned that healthy conflict wasn't possible, it would always end up with the person leaving the room or lashing out. At times, Gina's mom would hang up on her, telling her that she never wants to see her again. So, Gina took this into her relationships as well, assuming that if she dared to speak up and tell her partners that she would like them to change something, they too would yell at her and run away, leaving her abandoned, once again.

Unfortunately, this kind of behavior is not rare, far from it. This is something I see in my office more than any therapist wishes they had to. The way you were raised and whether you had the space to express your feelings and needs impacts whether you are capable of speaking out about your needs and wishes, and especially impacts how you view conflict. If sharing a boundary has always been associated with the other person losing it entirely or abandoning you, it's only natural that you will continue to have these thoughts in your relationships. However, learning that this is not the case is a step in the right direction.

If you struggle to set boundaries, remind yourself that these are normal, and needed, for any relationship to work. Tell yourself that you are deserving of respect. Tell yourself that you can express your thoughts and feelings, and that the right person will listen to you and will care. If you have a toxic partner, this lack of boundaries is something they appreciate, because it means that they can manipulate you into doing anything they want you to do. This is why boundaries are so important: they tell the person that there are things that you simply don't accept.

In a healthy relationship, your partner will be attentive. If you struggle to share these boundaries for reasons similar to Gina, take a minute to explain this to your partner. Tell them about how you feel and why you feel this way. Tell them that this is very difficult for you, and if you trust them, explain to them how you think this is going to go. Explaining this to a partner and making them understand why it is so difficult for you to speak up when something isn't working the way you want it to can help them get a better sense of how they can help you feel better and more respected. It can help them understand how they can be a good partner in this, and can show them that you might need to be reminded that they support you in this.

Your partner will also have boundaries, and chances are that they have already communicated a few of these with you. Try to think about these and see how you responded. Did you run away? Did you abandon them? Unless they crossed your boundaries, chances are that no, you didn't. That's because you are ready to adapt your ways of being and acting to ensure that the person in front of you feels safe. So, is it really all that hard to imagine that someone else could do this for you as well?

Setting Boundaries: The How-To to Get Started

Boundaries start with an I. They need to be representative of how you are feeling, and what you need, which means that you should focus on what you are thinking, instead of making it about the other person. For example, a boundary may be "I appreciate when my friends show up on time. I understand that some delays may happen, but I don't feel respected when I have to wait alone at a reserved table for thirty minutes because of a person's lack of punctuality." This boundary is based on your need and how another person's actions make you feel, instead of being about them changing their behavior. You are effectively highlighting a behavior that you do not appreciate and are showing what you would prefer instead. Now, if they want to abide by this or not is entirely their decision, and it is not something that you can change. All you can do is share how something makes you feel and hope that the person will understand this and do what they can to respect it.

Likewise, boundaries need to be made very clear. There is no place for a lack of clarity in boundary-setting, because the people you are sharing your boundaries with need to be clear about what you expect from them and why if you want them to be able to give you the kind of treatment you like. Otherwise, it just makes things confusing for others!

If your boundaries aren't respected or are being pushed back against, you have a few options. First, you need to stay calm, getting worked up or angry will bring in too much emotion, which can make it hard for you to stay clear on the why behind those boundaries. Likewise, you can (and potentially should) reassert your boundaries in case the person did not hear you correctly or did not understand exactly what you meant. Then, if none of this works, you have a choice to make: will you continue having this person in your life, or is this a deal breaker? Can you accept that they might not respect your boundaries, or is this something that you are refusing to deal with? There are different levels here. For example, you might accept that your friend might show up late a couple of times just because that's not something they are willing to work on. However, if you say a boundary about, for example, being spoken to respectfully by your partner, and they refuse to respect it and continue calling you names when you fight, or purposely call you names to upset you, this is not a boundary that is acceptable to cross as it reaches your self-esteem and value.

Consistency is also key with your boundaries. Your partner will expect consistency as otherwise, they may get confused, or may feel like they do not know what to do or how to act. If you feel like their behavior is unacceptable sometimes, but other times you laugh about it, try to pinpoint where the difference lies. Are there some jokes that feel disrespectful? If so, what about them is disrespectful, and what is the difference between this joke and the ones that you do find funny?

Your Partner Will Also Have Boundaries

Setting boundaries yourself is hard, but hearing others' boundaries can be just as hard. Take Gina, for example. For her, hearing her mother constantly telling her off made things confusing. What was okay one day would trigger a complete meltdown the next. Being told that her behavior was unacceptable wasn't just associated with her behavior, but with her specifically. She wasn't just doing something wrong, she was the wrong denominator in the situation. Therefore, she began to assume that being critiqued, being told that she is in the wrong, or being told that her behavior was unacceptable, always meant that she was disappointing, that she was wrong, and that she was the problem, not her behavior. As a result, whenever someone would tell her that she had done something slightly past the line of acceptable, she would take it personally and felt like it was a direct attack to her self-esteem and value as a human being. Can you guess how this went in the future, especially in relationships?

If you grew up in a similar environment, namely one in which you were constantly in the wrong, where you had to gauge the other person's reaction, and where you had to guess whether they would lash out or tell you something nicely, chances are that being told about someone's boundary can be equally triggering. You may feel like they are telling you that you have done something wrong, and therefore that you, as a person, aren't a good person or are failing to be a good person. You might feel anxious that this is the end of your relationship as in the past, being told that you had done something wrong ended with you being left on your own or abandoned by your parent while they lashed out.

In those moments, remind yourself that this is part of life. It's part of a relationship to have a partner tell us that they would like us to do something slightly different. Boundaries don't have to be said explicitly either! For example, your partner might kindly ask that you don't leave wet towels on the floor and that you, instead, put them in the hamper, it's a simple boundary, but nothing mean is meant by it. Likewise, you might want to try to pick up non-verbal cues as well that can show you that your partner has a specific boundary, like if they seem uncomfortable when you try to kiss them in public, or if they seem uncomfortable when you make jokes about their activity levels.

The key is to keep the conversation open and flowing. Have an open discussion with your partner and speak about your boundaries. Share how you feel about certain things and others. Be kind to each other, and remember that the goal is to have a relationship in which you both feel respected and cared for. This is a way for you two to express how certain actions or words make you feel, and to be on the same page. As always, communication is at the foundation of your trust!

Chapter Eight

Prioritizing Self-Care

You've learned how to set boundaries, so now, it's time to focus on your self-care. While your boundaries are there to help you protect yourself from people who may mean harm, to protect your feelings, and to ensure that your partner knows how to respect you in the way that you want to be respected, self-care is more about the respect that you show to yourself. In this day and age, we are constantly on the run. We are working non-stop to try and make ends meet. We are working hard to keep our social lives moving. We have kids, a family, a home to tend to, and a retirement to keep growing. Throughout all that, it can quickly feel overwhelming to also have to find some time to take care of ourselves. And yet, without it, we quickly approach a slippery slope towards burnout.

For us over thinkers, self-care is especially important because it forms the backbone of our mental and physical wellbeing. Without feeling good, without having time to ourselves to relax, we are much more prone to being stressed, anxious, and to keep overthinking things. Not only this, but when we feel like we are overwhelmed or stressed, we may need to be in control of something else to feel a sense of "having it together" so we look for ways to feel like that. One solution? To overthink and to try to find an explanation so we can better understand a situation.

Think about it. Have you ever been in a situation where everything around you feels like a chaotic mess? What do you tend to do? Some people freeze or get paralyzed in the mess. They feel like they can't move anymore. They're stuck there, unsure of what to do next. Others, however, have a different approach: they try to find control in places they think it could be hidden like their relationships. For example, if you are applying for jobs, need to move out soon because your lease is coming to an end soon, don't like your current job, and aren't sure of the future, you might turn to the one thing that's going well to get a sense of control: your relationship. You start overthinking, trying to grasp that control in any way you can. However, it doesn't always work out, in fact, usually, it just makes you even more anxious!

Self-Care to the Rescue

This is exactly why self-care is so important to avoiding overthinking. In the moments where you feel like you are not in control, like you don't know what's happening, and like everything is out of your hands, those are the moments when you need to focus on what you can do to calm yourself down. Those are the moments when you need to spend a bit of time with yourself and focus on how to reduce that amount of stress. Self-care will give you what you need; it's an individual activity that responds to your specific needs! In a way that helps you maintain stability in your mental and emotional health. It can be anything you may want to do as long as it detaches you from your daily stress and instead aligns you with your needs.

Self-care is especially helpful because it affects our overall well-being. It gives us a break in a life that can otherwise be extremely overwhelming, mainly because we rarely get to have a break unless we make a conscious effort to actively try to take care of ourselves. We are busy all the time, so much so that our time is usually spent taking care of other people's needs rather than our own. This is part of life to an extent, especially if you have kids, but to be the best person you can be, you also need to be in touch with yourself. You need to have time to relax, too. In fact, self-care has been shown to decrease anxiety and depression, and it can improve our relationships because it gives us the time and space we need to fulfill our own needs. Without filling our own cup first, it's much harder to fill other people's as well.

How Can I Self-Care?

You may have seen a lot of videos or general content online telling you that self-care is about getting your nails done, going to the spa, or taking a long bubble bath. And yet, while they are great ways to self-care, they won't necessarily be the right ones for you. As mentioned above, self-care is a very person-specific act, and it has to be an act that the person enjoys. If you feel like going to the gy for an hour is an act of self-care for you because it makes you feel good in your body, energizes you, and gives you some time to just be by yourself without having people calling you or asking for your help, then that might be your form of self-care. If you just need to have an hour in bed alone while reading a book, that works too. If you want to dedicate one day per month to go on a solo hike, that's a great self-care activity as well. The goal is to do something that helps you de-stress, and something that you like doing because it makes you feel good about yourself. Whether that's ironing, going for a swim, walking around when it is sunny, it doesn't matter, as long as it has the intended effect.

You might also want to try forms of self-care that especially help you stop overthinking. Try to think about the situations in which you overthink, and what the triggers are. If you can't think of it right now, go back to the previous few chapters we talked about this, as it may bring back some memories. Can you think of the reasons why you were overthinking? Now, think of things that could help distract you when this happens. For example, if you overthink when your partner's communication isn't great, you could do an activity where you need to leave your phone aside, like going swimming, or going hiking. If you feel like you need to ground yourself when this happens, you could also do some spring cleaning if it's something that helps relax you. Take a look at what your needs are and think of the ways that you could address these with activities and self-care habits.

Sometimes, you also just need a bit of downtime or time by yourself. If that is indeed the case, try something calmer such as journaling or meditation. These activities are simple, free of cost, and can be used for you to relax in an easy way. Don't focus on what you need to write, or on finding a way to self-care that is more extensive than just meditation or even writing. As long as it works for you, that's all that matters!

Integrate it into Daily Life

Self-care is not something you should only do when you are feeling down, when you need to relax, or when you have reached your limit. Instead, it should be seen as an opportunity for you to prevent bad feelings from coming up. It is a preventative method to help you counteract stressors that could trigger some overthinking patterns you might still have. So, make time for it! Schedule in some time for your self-care, and see it as something that you should do and something that you deserve to do, instead of something that you only get to do once everything else is done. Self-care should be seen as an important appointment. It's something that you should schedule into your day! Yes, it can be done on a daily basis, whether it's just taking 15 minutes to meditate every morning, writing in a gratitude journal, or having a night time routine that makes you feel really good right before you go to bed. This is a moment for you to focus on yourself while shutting out the rest, namely the things that do not need your attention right now. So, schedule it. Keep a few minutes aside each day for yourself.

Then, if you also want to spend a bit more time with yourself on a bigger activity, you can also schedule full self-care days where you just do whatever you want to do. Having these written down in your calendar will make them harder to skip, but it will also get rid of the guilt you might have around taking time for yourself. If you struggle to spend time on yourself because you feel like you have too many other things going on that are more urgent, making time for self-care might help you feel like it's okay to take some time off, and like it's okay to take time for yourself because that time won't be taking your energy or attention away from other things, it's all scheduled in.

This will also mean that you might have to get some boundaries going (yes, again!). You might need to learn to say no to requests that would take up your self-care time. Your self-care time isn't up for grabs and it's nonnegotiable, the same way a doctor's appointment is. It's a way for you to take care of yourself so you can avoid being overly stressed in the future, and so you can avoid falling into overthinking patterns. So, it's something that you should keep on prioritizing. If others want you to do something while you are self-caring, it's okay to say no and to explain that you are otherwise occupied. If you have children, it's something you can explain to them as well, focusing on how you need to have alone time too to be the best parent you can be. You can explain this to your partner as well so they understand more specifically why you need that alone time, and so they can help you have it if you need them to take up a few more tasks while you have your self-care time (and then, you can do the same for them when their time to self-care comes!).

If you have a hard time remembering to do it, use tools. In this day and age, we have all kinds of technologies and tools available to us. Have it written down in your Google Calendar or whichever online calendar you use. Remind yourself to drink water, track your sleep, use meditation tools, indeed, these are all forms of self-care, because they serve your most basic physiological needs.

Your Friends Can Add to Your Self-Care

You might feel like the time you spent socializing with friends is a good way to self-care. On the one hand, it is a good way to self-care because it helps us feel good about ourselves. We are surrounded by people who love us and who want what's best for us, who listen to us and who celebrate our milestones with us, but this is nonetheless not comparable to having time by ourselves. We need that alone time here and there to feel good. We need it to be able to do the things that we want to do without having to constantly focus on what others want us to do, or what we think others want. It might be awkward at first, especially if you are used to catering to everyone else's needs! In time, however, I guarantee you that you will learn to cherish the time you get to spend focusing on your needs and yourself.

Self-care doesn't need to be something you overthink about. Think of the things you like, take half an hour to plan out when you will do it on a daily basis and/or on occasional moments, and get started.

Chapter Nine

Embracing Imperfection and Growth

I have noticed a certain trend with people who come into a therapist's office to get support for their overthinking tendencies. Often, these stem from their upbringing, as we covered extensively throughout the past few chapters. Once this realization is made, once the client notices that their relationships have often followed the same pattern, dating someone either very healthy or very toxic, then the relationship not working out because of their lack of boundaries, their overthinking patterns, etc, there is a complete switch. It is as though they realize that before they can date again, they need to first address their own personal issues.

But it doesn't stop there. Once these issues are addressed and the person is able to set strong boundaries, a new sense of awareness emerges. This is both good and bad: in a way, it is a great development because the person is now capable of setting boundaries, can spot the signs of toxicity from miles ahead, and knows that they are worthy of being treated properly. However, it has some repercussions, including a sense of guilt and shame. They may look back to some of the friendships and relationships they have had in the past and feel regretful for their actions. They may have lost friendships over their people-pleasing behaviors, such as by cutting out friends who didn't abide by their shoulds and musts, instead of talking about them. They may have let go of perfectly good relationships with partners who were good to them because their overthinking patterns made them feel anxious and planted seeds of doubt in their minds, which over time killed the relationship. Thus, they feel guilty over their actions, regretful over the way they handled things, and they reach a new step in the therapy process: they need to forgive themselves.

In a way, one is grieving a past self. The person looks back on who they used to be and tends to feel like they aren't that person anymore. They feel ashamed of what they used to do, sometimes even so ashamed that they will avoid going back to certain places or doing certain things that they feel will bring those emotions back up. Forgiveness might be something we usually associate with other people, we forgive others and others forgive us, but in this process, forgiving yourself may very well be something that you need to do as well.

Let Go of Your Perfectionist Tendencies

If you relate to the former, this is something that you might need to start working on. It's difficult to look back on the things you have done in the past, the way your overthinking patterns may have hurt your current partner or even your relationship as a whole. You may have perfectionist tendencies in which you hold yourself responsible for always being perfect, and hence are really hard on yourself when you cannot live up to that expectation. You might even have moments when you feel like you are letting yourself and your partner down if you don't abide by the 'shoulds' of perfectionism. Your perfectionism might be manifesting as an unrealistic expectation of yourself or your partner, and you might be constantly trying to reach the unattainable ideal, which just makes you feel like you are never attaining it. Let go of that feeling. Accept that you aren't perfect, no one is. Accept that you have faults and that they make you who you are.

If these faults affect others, however, it is important to make sure that you do not simply accept that these are faults that others should cope with. If your perfectionist tendencies affect your partner because they also feel like they need to fit your view of perfection, you may end up with a partner who is constantly trying to meet your expectations, and may also have a partner who is deeply unhappy. Instead, accept that perfect doesn't exist. Understand that perfect will look different to every person you meet, and therefore, that your best is all that is needed.

So, set realistic expectations. Instead of having shoulds and musts that set you up for failure, know what is possible and what isn't. Know what you can do, and what you want to work towards. Importantly, accept that you might not always fulfill your own expectations. Likewise, focus on your strengths, instead of your flaws. Focus on what makes you the person you are, and what makes you incredible this way. Focus on what people say about you in a positive light, how do your friends describe you? Finally, appreciate the now. Think less about what happened or what might happen, and be present. What is happening right now? What facts do you have right now? What can you do right now? Part of this involves accepting yourself and your flaws. It means doing the work so you can forgive the things you did in the past, forgive yourself for what you may have done before you had therapy, and understand that with more self-awareness, you are now much better equipped to treat others in a way that you are proud of doing so.

It's Okay to Be Vulnerable

But it's hard. Part of embracing our imperfection and focusing on growth in the relationship includes having the ability to be vulnerable with ourselves and with our partner. We need to be authentic people if we want to have the real conversations with them, especially those that help us feel more comfortable in our relationships. Being vulnerable is a strength and not a weakness in a relationship, because opening up about your fears, your failures, and your insecurities deepens your emotional connection to one another. It helps you feel like you share these deep moments that lead you to trust each other. With this trust, it becomes easier for you to bring yourself back from a state of overthinking, because you can convince yourself that they are vulnerable with you and therefore want to share this side of themselves with you.

If this is something that feels like it could help you feel more comfortable in your relationship, and if it is something that could give you a better idea of where you stand as a couple (which can later help with your overthinking patterns), try asking your partner to do a few exercises to build vulnerability. For example, you can make it a habit to share something new about yourselves. You can make a pact that you will both express your needs openly from now on instead of trying to hide these or avoid talking about them altogether. You can also work on telling each other more about your deeper feelings so you feel like you can trust each other more, instead feeling like you need to wonder how your partner is feeling, which can trigger overthinking episodes.

Learn From Your Challenges

Part of your relationship's growth resides in your combined ability to learn from the challenges you have gone through. Every relationship has its own set of challenges, yours included. As an overthinker, you might have especially challenging moments when you feel like you can't share how you feel, can't tell your partner that you are anxious, and so on.

This might lead to conflicts, especially if your partner feels like they were excluded from the conversation. On the other hand, they may appreciate not having had to deal with the episode, especially if they can be disruptive to their day. This is a situation in which you could both learn from the challenge: your partner can highlight what they would prefer, and you can share with them how you feel about this and whether this is something you are comfortable with. The point here is that you can both learn from the challenges you go through and grow from this.

You are not only growing your relationship, you are also growing as a couple, as you feel more comfortable with one another, trust that you can say these things without a big blowout, and understand that your relationship needs to keep evolving alongside you for it to thrive.

You can learn from conflict too! If you have a conflict that feels especially productive or unproductive, try to pinpoint why that might be the case. Is there a reason why the conflict was more productive than usual? Did you both take time apart to think before you responded? Did you both make sure to listen to each other actively? Did you double-check things when you weren't sure you understood them correctly? Did you feel like your partner was kind and nice to you so you wouldn't overthink later on? On the other hand, if the conflict did not go well, what could you have done differently as a couple to make it work better? What was not good about it, and is this something you can change by yourselves, or will you need to get help from a therapist to fully understand what is at the root of this communication problem?

Take the challenges you face as a couple as a way for you to understand what you can do better both as a couple and as an individual. Take a good look at yourself and ask yourself whether you are communicating the right way, or whether you are letting your overthinking tendencies take over in these moments. Again, let go of the perfectionist side you have if you have it, and accept that it's okay to have these faults, as long as you are ready to act on them and to change things up to avoid them hurting your relationship.

Chapter Ten

Rebuilding Trust and Connection

As much as you may try to avoid overthinking, you might still have moments when you can't help it and fall into the trap all over again. These are the moments that will test your trust and connection, and they are some to cherish! They will be emotionally taxing, but they can still be used to make your relationship last longer and to strengthen the bond you have to your partner. Unfortunately, it's not uncommon for overthinking habits to come creeping up again even a few months or years after doing a lot of hard work to rid yourself of the habits. You might feel like you have dealt with them efficiently, but then something happens and boom! You are back into full-blown overthinking mode. These moments can feel like you are taking steps back in your relationship, but that's not the case. They are just hiccups to discuss with your partner, and

something to try and better understand so you can avoid
them later on.

Restoring Trust After Overthinking Episodes

So you have just had a moment of serious
overthinking. You're not sure what happened, but your head
feels fuzzy, you are overwhelmed by emotions, and you
don't know what to do about them. You feel incredibly
stressed, you don't know what you are thinking, you have a
hard time differentiating between what you are thinking and
what the reality is. You are in a full-blown overthinking
episode, and nothing seems to be able to hold you back. You
are trying to use your coping skills, but nothing works. So,
you revert to your old habits, asking your partner for more
reassurance, asking them to comfort you, asking them to
continue repeating the same things, I love you, yes we are
fine, no I'm not mad, etc. You know that they are getting
tired of it, but you can't help it, the what ifs are creeping up
again, and you feel like you don't have the coping skills you
need to overcome the thoughts.

So, a fight starts. You tell your partner all about
your thoughts. You might even blame them for things that
you think they are doing, when in reality, they have no idea
of what just happened. Then, the more you share, the more
you get that familiar feeling creeping in, you're

overwhelmed by your thoughts and you don't know how to differentiate between what you were thinking and what actually happened. Your partner, trying to calm you down and process the situation, might be more focused on making you feel better than trying to come to a conclusion or common ground. The result? A conflict situation that might make you feel guilty and ashamed later, and that probably adds fuel to your overthinking 'fire' because you then feel like you have just started problems where there aren't any.

How do you get past this as a couple? Well, the steps are similar to the 12-step program for A.A. You start by acknowledging what you did and the fact that it had an impact on your partner. Use "I" to describe how you feel, instead of saying you, which might come across as being aggressive or may make your partner feel like they need to defend themselves. Share your emotions without placing any blame on the other person, but also accept responsibility for your role in this, as your partner should not be the one in charge of making you feel better if you were responsible for the miscommunication between the two of you. Then, start working on building trust again. You need to apologize if you have hurt your partner. Then, you need to reaffirm your commitment to one another.

You also have work to do on your end. You need to think about what triggered this emotion in you and what you will do in the future to address this (i.e., to avoid being triggered). Trust can be rebuilt if your partner feels like you know where things went wrong and if you show the ability to address this trigger. Of course, your partner should also support you in this, such as by ensuring that they do what they can, within reason, of course, to help you avoid these triggers. For example, if their communication triggered it and it was indeed lacking, they can address this. However, if the overthinking stemmed from an irrational place and you know that your partner isn't to blame, this is something to acknowledge to ensure that they don't feel responsible for something that doesn't belong to them.

Transparency and Consistency

Acknowledging your faults will be necessary for full transparency and consistency, and hence, to rebuild the trust that might be slightly broken between the two of you. Be transparent with your partner about how you feel when you overthink, and try to come to terms with a way that they can help you when you feel these triggers come up. It belongs to you to do the work to avoid anxiety and to address it, but that doesn't mean that you are alone in your fight. It just means that you have to be transparent with how you are feeling so your partner can help you the best way they can.

Trust can also be rebuilt through transparency on a daily basis. Share your plans with each other. Say good morning and good night every day. Keep it consistent so both partners feel comfortable and at peace in the relationship. Consistency in actions, words, and emotional support confirms reliability and commitment, helping both you and your partner feel like you can be vulnerable and trust each other.

Forgive and Heal

Unfortunately, overthinking can leave some scars in a relationship. Although the overthinker might feel like their partner has it easier because they don't have to deal with trust issues, it can be taxing for the person who is dating the overthinker to feel like they are constantly being scrutinized or constantly need to reaffirm their partner. This is something that may require you to forgive yourself, and your partner to forgive you. Over time, if overthinking isn't addressed, it's only normal for your partner to feel like they are stuck in a situation where no matter what they do, they are constantly trying to avoid triggering you. So, forgiveness can come, but it will come faster if you put in the work to make it easier for your partner to feel like you are giving it your all.

For your relationship to work, you need to be able to forgive yourselves for the mistakes you might have made. Otherwise, hanging onto these thoughts and feelings might just keep you both stuck in a cycle in which you think non-stop about what happened before and struggle to move on from it. Your relationship should be moving forward, and for this, you must be able to stop looking at past events and focus, instead, on what can happen in the future if you work as a team to make this happen.

Let Go of Resentment!

You are in a relationship with this person, which means that you still love and care for them. However, it doesn't mean that you will never struggle with resentment, especially if you feel like you are dealing with things that they have never had to deal with before. If you feel resentful towards them because they do not seem to understand what you are experiencing, you need to let these feelings go and need to focus on rebuilding trust with one another. Likewise, if you feel resentment over things that have happened in the past with them, if you have chosen to stay with them, you need to be able to accept this and to move forward without this resentment.

You also need to be willing to let go of the resentment you might be feeling towards yourself. Having read this book now nearly to completion, you may have had quite a few moments where you thought, wow, that's SO me. If so, you might have also had a rude awakening that you need to confront your overthinking patterns if they have been affecting your relationship. You might feel resentful of your past actions or the things you did in your relationship, and you might feel resentful of how you, for example, handled conflict before. Again, you need to forgive yourself and have to look ahead. Accept that these are mistakes that have been made, and accept that you cannot change this. All you can do is move forward and make sure not to make these mistakes again.

Move Forward with Compassion and Understanding

We are all human beings. We all make mistakes. We all do things that we regret. This includes me as well! We all have moments we look back on, cringe internally inside, and feel uncomfortable about. However, if you want to move forward and overcome overthinking, you have to be ready to accept that this is part of your past and that you didn't know any better. A motto I like is "I did what I could with the resources I had in the context I was in." We do things the way we think we should do them. We don't intentionally do things to hurt people (hopefully!). So, when things go wrong, when we hurt people, we need to be able to accept responsibility, apologize, and move forward.

Be compassionate towards yourself. Be understanding of where you come from, the changes you have been working on, and what you want to do differently in the future. Show yourself some grace and be kind to yourself. Avoid speaking negatively about yourself or your past, and instead, accept that this was a part of your life that happened, and thankfully, one that you chose to do differently so you could feel better about yourself and your relationships.

And if it happens again, don't be so hard on yourself. Old habits die hard, and they might require you to keep working hard at them to truly get rid of them. But don't worry, it is worth the hard work!

Conclusion

I have always found it an interesting idea that our brains somehow manage to overdo what they do best, think. Overthinking is a peculiar thing, something that doesn't make rational sense, and yet, it is also something that can truly take a toll on a person's life. We have seen just how much of a toll it can take throughout the past few pages, and perhaps you can vouch for that yourself through your personal experiences.

Nevertheless, the goal of this book was not to simply tell you about overthinking or to educate you on the mechanisms behind it. It was, instead, to teach you how to get control of it once and for all. As a therapist, I have seen time and time again how overthinking can seriously hurt relationships, it erodes the trust, exhausts both people, makes the overthinker feel like they are going crazy, and the other partner like they don't know what to do to make the other feel more secure. It's a complex thing, overthinking, but it's something that you can overcome with the right tools.

These tools are the main ones we discussed throughout this book, including understanding why you have the attachment style that you have, how this style affects your relationships, identifying the triggers that affect you most significantly, and addressing these triggers. It additionally includes being aware of your negative thought patterns and changing them so they are more fruitful and conducive to well-being, as well as having strong boundaries (and learning how to set them because let's face it, they can be tough to communicate!).Then, there's also self-care, which is needed as a preventative method to help you cope with the stressful moments so you can avoid large triggers.

You may notice that once you go through these steps, you start looking back on past versions of yourself and feel like this was a different person. This is not uncommon, in fact, many people feel this way after going through therapy. You might feel ashamed of your previous actions, or even more deeply ashamed of how you used to view yourself, speak to yourself, and treat yourself. In those moments, remember that being empathetic towards yourself is better than any negative comment you can make about yourself. You're someone who, like other people, experienced growth, that's something positive and something to celebrate. So, be kind to yourself. Show yourself some empathy. Remind yourself that you are allowed to change and to better yourself. Do this journey with your partner, and celebrate your milestones together, the growth is definitely worth celebrating.

On that note, this is where I leave you. I truly hope that this book brought you the help and support you needed in one way or another. These are topics and concepts to continue exploring, so I encourage you to consider therapy if this is something that you feel may be helpful to your specific case.

Having said this, I wish you the very best in the remainder of your journey.